Paper Piecing the Seasons

Foundation Piecing from Easy to Expert

Martingale
& COMPANY

Liz Schwartz & Stephen Seifert

Dedication

The ease and accuracy of foundation piecing has introduced a whole new generation to the joys of quilting. There is nothing as rewarding as seeing the happiness and confidence that lights up a new quilter's face after they've completed only one foundation pieced project. We dedicate this book to all of our quilting friends, old and new, who have touched our lives.

Credits

Technical Editor .... Ursula Reikes
Text Designer .... Liz Schwartz
Design Coordinator .... Stephen Seifert
Production Associate .... Jim Murphy

Zippy Designs Publishing
Home of *The Foundation Piecer*
RR 1 Box 187M
Newport, VA 24128
www.foundationpiecer.com

Martingale & Company
PO Box 118
Bothell, WA 98041-0118

Printed in Hong Kong
03 02 01 00   10 9 8 7 6 5 4

Library of Congress Cataloging-in-Publication Data

Schwartz, Liz
    Paper piecing the seasons : foundation piecing from easy to expert / by Liz Schwartz and Stephen Seifert.
    p. cm.
    ISBN 1-56477-248-9
    1. Patchwork—Patterns. 2. Machine quilting—Patterns.
I. Seifert, Stephen. II Title.
TT835.S3489 1998
746.46—dc21   98-41144
                                CIP

Table of Contents

Preface

Foundation piecing is steeped in tradition. For centuries, quilters have stitched their precious fabric scraps to pieces of canvas, muslin, magazine and newspaper pages, even old parchment. The foundation material, whether fabric or paper, provided a stable base for patchwork blocks. In the past, only a handful of designs were made using the foundation piecing method. Today, quilters use foundations to sew myriad designs—if you can draw it, you can piece it on paper or fabric.

Foundation piecing allows novice quilters to sew difficult patterns quickly and easily, and offers seasoned quilters a means to explore and develop their creativity. Not only can foundation piecing be used to create masterful renditions of traditional quilt patterns, but it can also be used to create stunning pictorial quilts with ease and precision.

Introduction

Quilting is a way of sharing our love with those we hold dear to our hearts. Whenever we take time out of our ever growing, busy schedules to make a special gift for someone we love, it truly expresses how much we care. These treasured keepsakes are what we pass down from generation to generation and cherish in our hearts.

As the seasons progress, changes in our surroundings mark important celebrations and provide endless ideas for quilting projects. Who cannot be inspired by the beauty of new-fallen snow blanketing the countryside, or by the glowing crimson foliage of trees preparing for a winter's nap? Nature is a driving force in our lives, so it seems only fitting that our quilts should reflect our experiences.

The goal of this book is to introduce the foundation piecing technique and explore some of the possibilities of this wonderfully fast and accurate method. With every project that you finish, you develop and build upon your foundation piecing skills. It is our belief that after completing only four projects, one from each of the major sections, you will have become an expert foundation piecer. We hope that after seeing how easy it is to piece even the most intricate pictorial quilt, you will be empowered to conquer any foundation pieced project. We wish you many joyous holidays and pleasurable hours of stitching beautiful quilted creations.

Foundation and Paper Piecing

One of the most common questions we hear is, "What is the difference between paper and foundation piecing?" Paper piecing, the process of stitching fabric patches to paper foundations, is a form of foundation piecing. The term *foundation piecing* is more inclusive, as it also refers to piecing done on any foundation material, including paper, fabric, interfacing, and canvas. Since you can use any foundation material you wish to complete these quilt projects, we will refer to the process throughout this book as *foundation* piecing rather than *paper* piecing.

While we prefer to use only cotton fabrics in our quilts, it should be noted that one of the advantages of fabric foundation piecing is that it allows you to use fabrics that would generally be considered unsuitable for quilts. Since a fabric foundation is not removed when the patchwork blocks are completed, it serves as a permanent stabilizer for silk, lamé, wool, satin, lace, and other delicate fibers.

The Intimidation Factor

All the projects in this book can be made by anyone familiar with sewing. You do not have to be an expert quilter or seamstress to make beautiful quilts. The most crucial stumbling blocks for quilters who want to create beautiful foundation pieced pictorial quilts are their own preconceptions, or what we refer to as "the intimidation factor." Often, the most common reaction to an intricate piece is, "Wow! It's gorgeous but *I* could never make that." The first step to completing a quilt is having the courage to start. So, don't be intimidated; it's really not as difficult as it looks!

Creating the Fabric Palette

Just as an artist needs a palette of paints and supplies, a quilter needs an assortment of fabrics in varying scales, textures, and colors. While almost any type of fabric can be used for foundation piecing, we prefer 100% cotton. Like a painting, the completed scene will be composed of different areas of color. Since the piecework creates the picture, the main job of the fabric is to bring the pieced scene to life.

When selecting fabrics for pictorial foundation pieced quilts, you must consider that the role of the fabric is to enhance the dramatic effect of the scene. Try to envision how the texture and feel of a print will influence your final piece and make it more exciting. Don't worry about matching all of the fabrics; let the overall look and feel of the scene guide you.

❧ *Feature Print:* Pick a fabric that you love, or one that reflects the theme of the finished quilt. Since this print will usually be used only in the border, it should be a medium- to large-scale print that contains as least five or more colors. When selecting the remaining colors for the project, use the feature print as a guide. Note that your companion prints do not have to be exact color matches. Often, using complementary and contrasting colors adds interest to the finished quilt. Remember, the feature print is only a guide for choosing coordinates, so don't let it hinder your creativity.

Feature Prints

Since this fabric will be used only in the border, it should be a medium- to large-scale print that contains at least five or more colors.

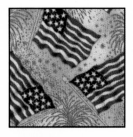

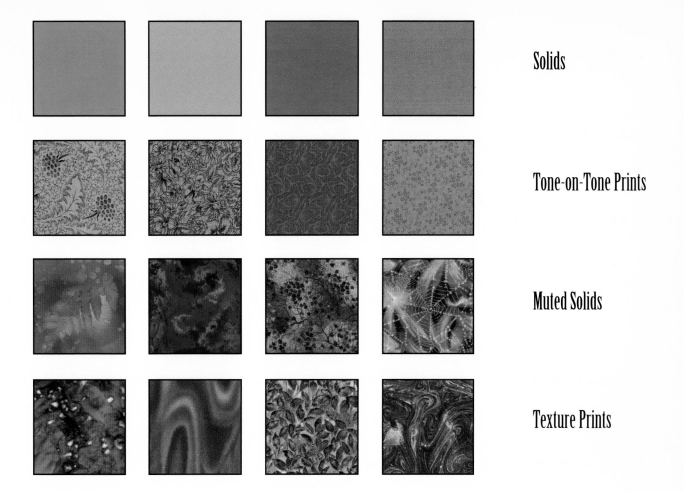

Solids

Tone-on-Tone Prints

Muted Solids

Texture Prints

Solids: One-color fabrics with no visible printed design, solids are excellent filler fabrics and are best used in tiny pieces where a printed design might be lost. Use only one or two solid fabrics in the quilt.

Tone-on-Tone Prints: These fabrics "read" as one color and usually consist of a solid-colored fabric overprinted with a shade or tint of the background color. Tone-on-tone prints are an indispensable addition to your fabric palette and are good for filling in color gaps.

Muted Solids: Contrary to the name, the fabrics in this grouping are not solids. While a muted solid is monochromatic, it contains three or more shades or tints of the same hue. The additional shades add dimension to the print and help create the illusion of perspective in the finished quilt.

Texture Prints: Containing more than one color, texture prints have an overall design that suggests the surface has tactile properties. Good examples of fabrics with texture are hand-dyed and painted fabrics as well as marbled designs. Texture prints help make the pieced scene seem three-dimensional.

Color Terminology

Hue is another word for color.

Monochromatic describes a color scheme that uses several shades or tints of one hue.

A *shade* is a darker variation of a color.

A *tint* is a lighter variation of a color.

Some quilts use subtle value distinctions. When a *pale* fabric is listed, choose a value that is lighter than your *light* fabric.

7

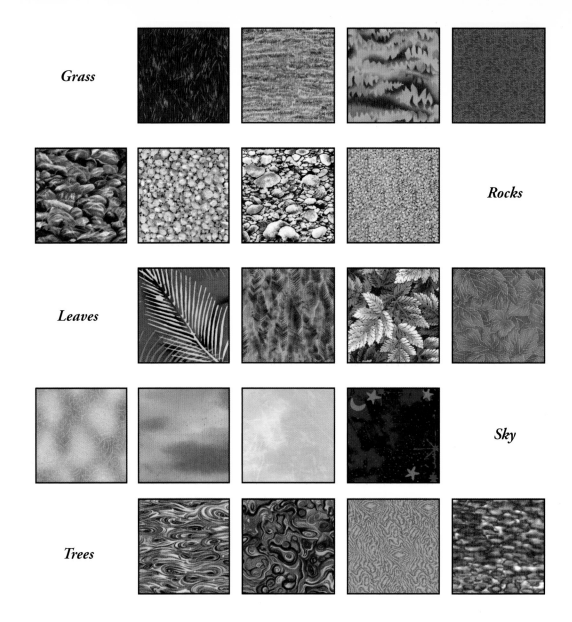

Grass

Rocks

Leaves

Sky

Trees

❧ *Natural Elements:* There are many wonderful fabrics available that represent natural elements like grass, rocks, water, trees, leaves, and sky. Using one or more of these prints really adds sparkle to the finished quilt because they add an important element of realism that other fabrics may not adequately portray.

Mixing the Colors

Now that we have defined our palette, we need a way to arrange the fabrics so that they will make a pleasing composition. Remember that these guidelines are meant to be a rough framework and should not be followed with a rigidity that does not allow spontaneity.

⤚ *One fabric should be a feature print.*
      The feature print sets the tone for the project. Use it to help determine the other colors you'll use.

⤚ *Approximately one-third of the fabrics should be texture prints.*
      Texture prints add dimension and depth to the quilt.

⤚ *The remaining two-thirds should be a combination of muted solids, natural elements, solids, and tone-on-tone prints.*
      These fabrics fill in color gaps and are the building blocks of the quilt.

Foundation Piecing Basics

Gathering and
arranging your
materials before you
start sewing is the
key to a successful
and enjoyable
project.

When stitching
pictorial quilts,
make two copies of
all the foundations
needed. Then color
one set with colored
pencils and tape the
entire project
together following
the project
directions. Use this
full-size mock-up as
a guide for sewing
and color placement.
Use the other set for
stitching.

Supplies

- Wooden seam pressing bar
- Add-A-Quarter template ruler
- Sewing machine
- Iron and ironing board
- Flannel press cloth
- Size 90/14 sewing machine needles
- Sewing thread
- Rotary cutter and mat
- Rotary rulers: 6" x 24" and 12½" x 12½"
- Vinyl-coated paper clips
- Sewing pins
- Tweezers (for removing paper)
- Cotton fabrics in desired colors

Foundation Materials

• *Fabric:* When you want your foundation to be permanent, you can transfer it to fabric by tracing or by using an iron-transfer fabric pen. This foundation will add stability to the finished piece. However, it should be noted that the extra layer may make hand quilting more difficult. Suitable fabrics include muslin, polyester-cotton blends, and nonwoven interfacing (or used dryer sheets).

• *Paper:* Just about any type of paper will make a suitable foundation. It is advisable to test the paper first to make sure that it handles well and does not fall out prematurely or shrink when ironed. We like Easy Piece foundation paper: it is translucent and easy to remove from the finished project. Other suitable papers include typing paper, onion skin, vellum, copy paper, tracing paper, tissue paper (use caution when using this material; it is extremely delicate), parchment, and freezer paper.

Left to right:
photocopy on
paper, iron-on
transfer on muslin,
needle-punch on
Easy Piece
foundation paper,
photocopy on
tracing paper.

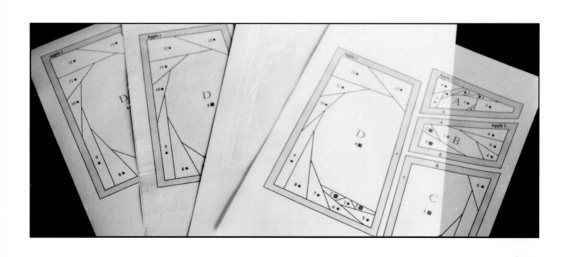

Preparing the Foundations

• *Needle Punching:* Multiple foundations can be made quickly and accurately with this technique. First, trace the foundation pattern onto a piece of tracing paper. Layer the traced pattern with up to ten sheets of the desired foundation paper. Then, with an unthreaded sewing machine, sew along the traced lines. Repeat until you have enough foundations for the project.

• *Photocopying:* All photocopiers distort images to some degree. Because of this, we recommend that you test the accuracy of the machine (see note at right) before copying foundations for large multiple-block or pictorial quilts. If you find that the machine does not significantly distort the foundations, then this method is the fastest and most inexpensive way to reproduce foundation patterns. If you do photocopy your foundations, make sure to always photocopy from the same original and make all of the copies for the project on the same machine.

• *Tracing:* Although time-consuming, tracing is an effective and accurate way to reproduce foundation patterns. A clear advantage to this technique is that it eliminates distortion.

Cutting

When preparing materials for a foundation pieced quilt, first gather all the foundations and supplies for the entire project. Then, using the color guide for the project, label each corresponding fabric with its name and color symbol to help avoid confusion when you sew the foundation units.

Rather than cutting out the shape of the finished piece, as you would for traditional patchwork, cut fabric strips of varying widths and use them to piece the foundation sections.

• Starting with the first color, look through all of the foundation sections for the project and determine the largest piece that will need to be cut.

• Measure the widest section of the piece and add ¾" to that number. This extra room in the seam allowances ensures that the fabric patch will cover the entire area it is supposed to.

• Cut a strip of fabric to the width of the measurement.

• Rough cut the fabric patches from the strip as needed. If you need more fabric strips, repeat the steps above.

• Continue cutting fabric strips for all the colors required in the project. Remember to be generous with your cutting. Even though this method may waste some fabric, it makes the whole project much more enjoyable and fun. It can be very frustrating to find that in an effort to save fabric, you cut the patch ⅛" too short and will have to rip it out and resew.

Photocopy Check

To test the accuracy of a photocopier, make one copy of the pattern on the machine. Place the copy over the original and hold the papers up to a light source. You will be able to see how closely the copy matches the original. If the copy is significantly different from the original, choose another machine or another technique to make your foundation patterns.

Measuring the foundation to determine proper strip size

11

Preparing to Sew

Prepare your sewing machine by reducing the stitch length to 18 to 20 stitches per inch and changing your needle to a size 90/14. Replace the needle every time you start a new project. Also, be sure not to use steam when ironing as this may cause the foundation to shrink or distort.

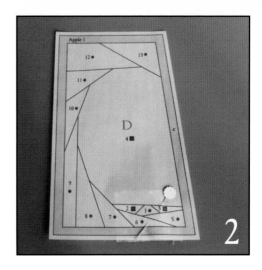

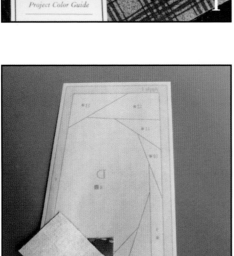

Sewing the Foundation Units

1.   Carefully read all the directions for the project you have chosen. Then, using your favorite method, prepare all the foundations you will need. Arrange and cut all the necessary fabric strips and patches. Be sure each fabric strip is labeled with the color and symbol it corresponds to in the project color guide.

2.   Place your first fabric piece right side up on the wrong (unprinted) side of your first paper foundation. Check to see if the fabric will cover the area by holding up the paper and the fabric to a light source (printed side of foundation facing you). Make sure that the fabric covers the entire area! Pin or glue (using a dab of glue from a glue-stick) in place.

3.   Place the second piece of fabric right side down on top of the first. Position the fabric so that it extends approximately ¼" past the sewing line, and pin in place. Hold the foundation and fabric up to a light source so that you can see the sewing line and check that the piece is positioned correctly. Hold the fabric in place and flip it over so you can see if it covers the entire area, including seam allowances.

4. Flip the foundation (with the fabrics in place) to the printed side and sew on the line between the first and second pieces. Extend your line of stitching at least ¼" before and after the printed line (this helps prevent the seams from ripping out).

5. Fold the fabric into place. To protect your ironing board from the ink on the foundation papers, cover it with a flannel press cloth. Place the foundation, paper side down, on the cloth, then press gently with an iron. Be sure not to touch the printed side of the foundation with your iron. Do not use steam, as this may distort the finished unit. Or, you can use a wooden seam pressing bar to press the seams and make them lie flat.

6. Align a postcard or straight edge along the next sewing line. Crease the paper and fold it over the postcard to reveal the fabric patch below.

7. Place an Add-A-Quarter ruler on the crease so that the ¼" lip is pushed against the crease, then trim the excess fabric, leaving a ¼" seam allowance. Alternatively, you could use a regular rotary ruler for this step; just be sure to trim ¼" from the crease.

8. Align the next piece along the trimmed edge. Continue adding patches in order until the foundation is covered.

Ruler Tip

If you cannot find the Add-A-Quarter ruler in your favorite quilt shop, you can make your own! Simply take a rotary ruler and ¼"-wide quilter's masking tape. Then, using multiple layers of tape, build a lip on the underside of the ruler between the edge and the ¼" mark.

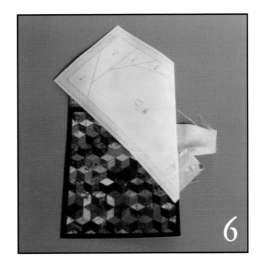

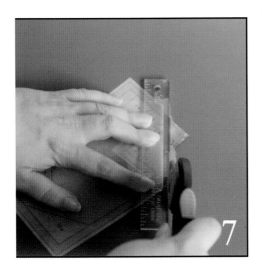

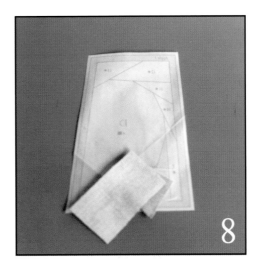

9. Using a small stitch, baste around the entire foundation within the ¼" seam allowance. Be careful that the basting doesn't extend into the visible areas of the foundation section (past the inner sewing line).

10. After the block is completed, trim the excess fabric and paper from the foundation; be sure to cut on the outer solid line. Do not remove the paper from the blocks until they have been assembled and you are ready to quilt the project.

Assembling the Foundation Units

Now that all the foundation units have been completed, it's time to put them together. Gather the foundation sections and check to see that you've really completed all the units.

The Assembly Diagram for the project is a visual map that shows how the sections fit together to make the design. It is important to note that the Assembly Diagram shows the foundations from the *printed side* and that the fabric side will be the mirror image of what is shown. Even though it may seem intuitive to flip the foundations over and look at the fabric side, all of the assmebly steps are best done looking only at the printed side of the foundation.

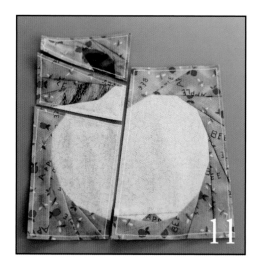
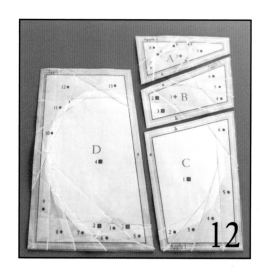

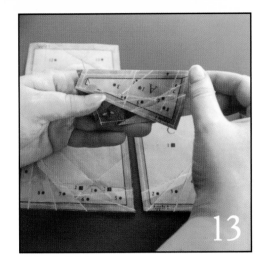

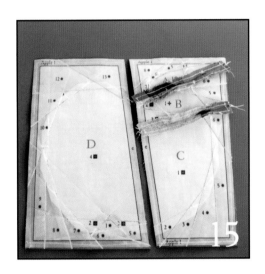

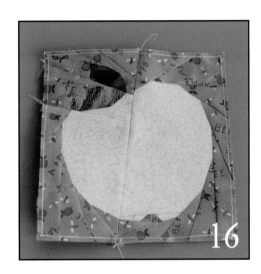

11. Arrange the completed foundation sections with the printed side facing you, as shown in the Project Assembly Diagram. Flip the sections over to the fabric side and check to see if you made any mistakes while sewing the units.

12. Flip the units back to the printed side. Locate the lowercase letters in the seam allowances of the foundations. Matching *a* to *a*, sew the sections together.

13. Identify several key match points (such as ends and center seams) and place pins through them so that the pins pass perpendicularly through the sewing lines (the inner line on the paper foundation) of both blocks. Align the sections, matching pins, then fasten them together using several vinyl-coated paper clips.

14. After the paper clips are set, remove all of the pins. Sew the units together, removing the paper clips as you sew. Press the seams open to reduce bulk.

15. Continue sewing sections together in alphabetical order, matching lowercase letters.

16. Assemble the completed subunits to make the pieced scene.

Batting

Many types of batting are available to quilters today. You can choose from silk, wool, cotton, polyester, or combinations of different fibers. While we prefer a 100% cotton batting for a soft, old-fashioned feel, almost any type of batting can be used successfully in a foundation pieced quilt. However, you may want to avoid very high loft battings becasue it's difficult to quilt them without introducing wrinkles into the pieced top.

Removing the Paper

17. When the quilt top has been completed, remove the paper foundations from the back of the blocks. If you have trouble removing the paper, try using a pair of tweezers to get into the tight spots. Moistening the paper, or gently scraping it with your fingernail, also helps coax difficult pieces to come off. You might even try soaking the whole piece in water—when the paper gets wet, it will fall right off. However, be careful not to clog your sink or washing machine with paper. If you used muslin foundations, remember that they will not be removed and will become a permanent part of the quilt.

Assembling the Quilt Sandwich

18. To prepare your top for quilting, layer it with batting and backing and then baste the layers together. First, cut a piece of batting that is at least 1" larger than the quilt top on all sides, then cut the backing fabric 1" larger than the batting on all sides. Using masking tape, tack the backing to a flat surface with the wrong side facing up. The fabric should be taut, but be careful not to pull it out of shape. Lay the batting on the backing, then place the quilt top face up on the batting and carefully smooth out any wrinkles.

19. Starting in the center of the quilt, baste the layers together. Cover the entire surface of the quilt with basting, leaving no more than a 4" space between the lines. To baste with thread, use a long darning (or doll-making) needle and systematically work outward from the center in a grid. (See photo 19a, page 16.) If you prefer, you can baste with large safety pins. (See photo 19b, page 16.) If you use pins, make sure that they are rust-resistant so they won't leave marks on your quilt. To save your fingers, you can use a spoon to close the pins.

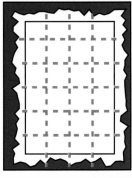

Basting grid pattern

Quilting

20. Because most foundation pieced quilts have many seams, some areas of the pieced top may be very thick. This bulkiness makes hand quilting difficult, so we almost exclusively machine quilt our projects. Outlining the main structural features of the pattern by quilting "in the ditch" is a good way to highlight the design. Another possibility is to use an overall stipple or geometric quilting pattern.

21. After you have completed quilting the project, remove any remaining basting threads or safety pins. When removing basting threads, be careful not to pull out the quilting stitches. Also, trim off all of the thread tails left from machine quilting.

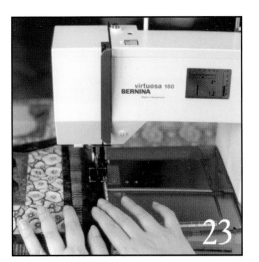

Binding

22. To prepare binding for your quilt, measure the total length of all sides of the quilt and add an extra 16" to the measurement. Cut enough 2½"-wide strips across the crosswise grain of the fabric to equal the measurement. To join the strips, layer them right sides together and use a diagonal seam. (See photo 22, page 17.) Trim the seam to ¼" and press it open. Fold the strips in half with wrong sides together, aligning the cut edges, and press.

23. Starting about ⅓ of the way from a corner, align the raw edge of the binding with the quilt. Using a walking foot, begin stitching at least 4" from the end of the binding and continue until you are ¼" from the corner. (See photo 23, page 17.)

24. At the ¼" point, stop sewing and backstitch.

25. Fold the binding straight up from the corner so that it forms a 45° angle.

26. Fold the binding strip down so that the raw edge is aligned with the edge of the quilt, and continue sewing from the top of the corner.

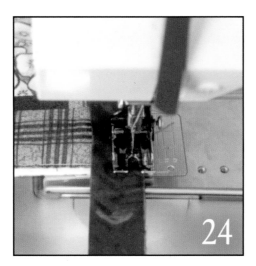

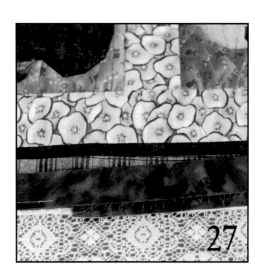

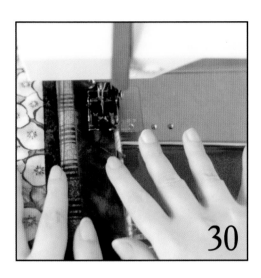

27. Stop sewing at least 9" from the point where you started to attach the binding; make sure that you have at least a 7" tail of binding remaining after you stop stitching.

28. To join the two free ends of the binding strip, place one of the tails inside the other and smooth out the wrinkles so they both lie flat. Keeping the tails together, lift and fold them to form a 45° angle as shown above. Lightly press the fold with an iron.

29. Open the tails and place them right sides together. Align the crease at the lower edge of the top strip with the crease on the bottom strip. Sew on the crease, continuing diagonally to the opposite corner. Trim the seam allowance to ¼" and press it open.

30. Fold the binding into position and finish sewing the seam.

31. Bring the binding to the back of the quilt, covering the stitching lines, and whipstitch the edge in place.

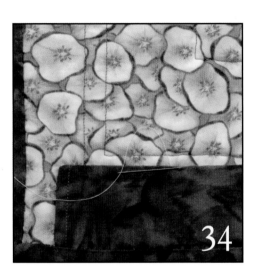

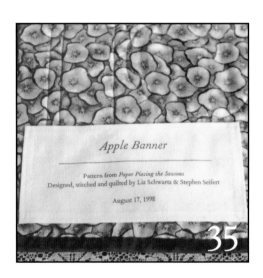

Attaching a Hanging Sleeve

32. Cut a 5½"-wide strip of fabric that is 1" shorter than the width of your finished quilt. Hem the short edges of the strip.

33. With wrong sides together, sew the long edges of the strip together to form a tube. Open the tube and fold it so that the seam is centered on the back; press the seam open.

34. Whipstitch the finished sleeve to the back of the quilt.

Signing Your Quilt

35. Sign and date the back of your quilt. If desired, cut a separate patch of fabric, sign and date the patch, and then applique it to the backing fabric.

Winter

Snow Crystals Bed Quilt

Valentine Angel

Country Cottage

Snow Crystals Bed Quilt

Finished Size: 84" x 96"
Block Size: 12" x 12"
Rating: Easy

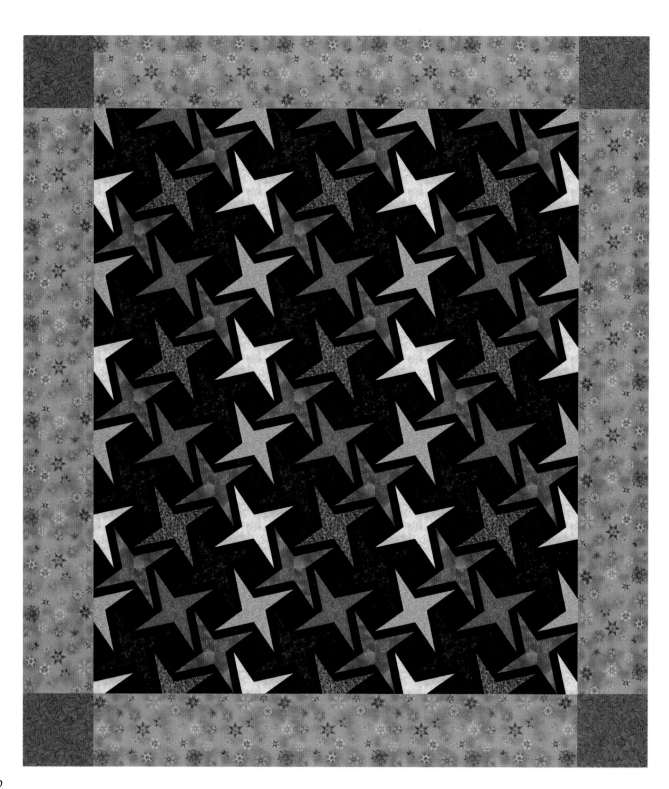

Foundation Coloring Diagram
(view from printed side of foundation)

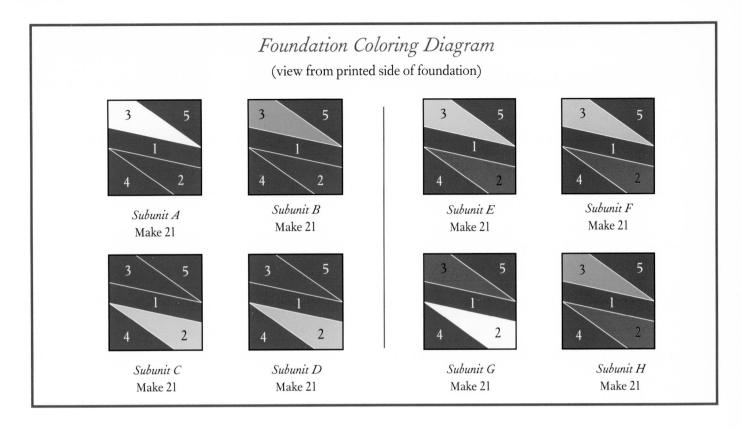

Subunit A
Make 21

Subunit B
Make 21

Subunit E
Make 21

Subunit F
Make 21

Subunit C
Make 21

Subunit D
Make 21

Subunit G
Make 21

Subunit H
Make 21

It is no wonder why we decided to start this book with this marvelous project, *Snow Crystals Bed Quilt*. A great introduction to the foundation piecing technique, this easy quilt is a fast and fun project. While the quilt shown uses a repeating-color star pattern, you could easily give it a scrappy look by making each star different.

This seasonal block is a real treat, and you don't have to shovel any snow to enjoy it! The quilt is made by constructing two blocks that are tiled. After completing this project, you will have mastered the basics of foundation piecing and will be ready to move on to the next step.

Materials (based on 40"-wide fabric)
9 yds. grape

2 yds. light gray green

2 yds. tan

2 yds. lavender

2 yds. dusty pink

2¾ yds. moss green

2¾ yds. mauve

2½ yds. border print

Cutting (for outside borders)
From the lengthwise grain of the border print, cut four 6½" x 84½" strips.

Assembly
1. Make 168 copies of the *Snow Crystals Bed Quilt* foundation. Using the Foundation Coloring Diagram as a guide, mark each foundation with the color and subunit designation shown. Remember that the diagram shows the foundations from the printed side, so simply mark each color in the numbered spot on the foundation pattern.

Block Assembly Diagram
(view from printed side of foundation)

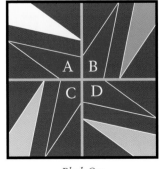

Block One
Make 21

Block Two
Make 21

23

2. Sew 21 each of subunits A–H.

3. Arrange subunits A–D as shown in the Block Assembly Diagram to make Block One. Sew the units together to make 21 Block One.

4. Arrange subunits E–H as shown in the Block Assembly Diagram to make Block Two. Sew the units together to make 21 Block Two.

Putting It All Together

1. Arrange the completed blocks as shown in the Project Assembly Diagram, alternating Block One and Two units.

2. Sew the blocks together to make seven rows of six blocks each. Sew the rows together.

Borders

Starting with the long sides of the quilt, sew one border strip to each side. Attach the remaining strips to the top and bottom of the quilt top.

Finishing

1. Remove the paper from the back of the quilt top.

2. Layer the quilt top with batting and backing; baste.

3. Machine quilt with silver metallic thread to add sparkle. If desired, quilt a simple snowflake design in the border.

4. Bind the quilt and add a hanging sleeve.

5. Sign and date your quilt.

Project Assembly Diagram
(view from printed side of foundation)

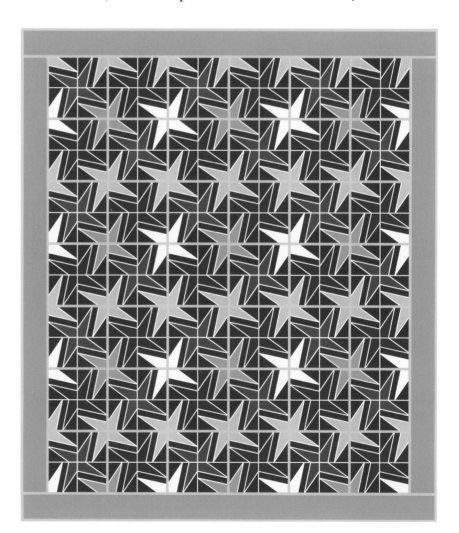

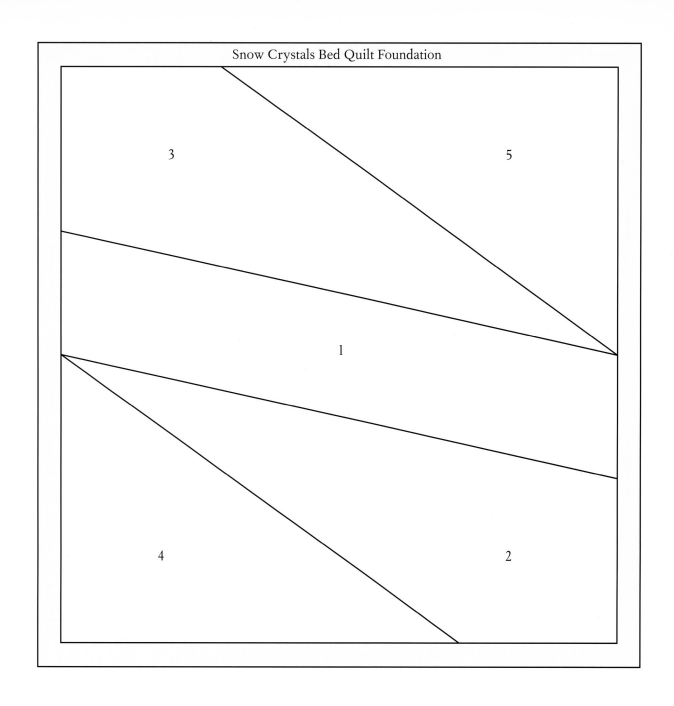

Snow Crystals Bed Quilt Foundation

Make 168 copies

Valentine Angel

Finished Size: 18" x 24"
Rating: Easy

O that 'twere possible
After long grief and pain
To find the arms of my true love
Round me once again!
~ Alfred, Lord Tennyson ~

Love is the strongest emotion that we can ever experience. It opens our hearts and minds to new and wonderful worlds!

As springtime approaches, our affections begin to swell. It is not surprising that our sweethearts are the targets of our tender feelings. So why not send Valentine greetings to *your* sweetheart with this charming quilt. This wall hanging's sweet angel hovers in a heart as she sings hymns of love to your Valentine.

Materials *(based on 40"-wide fabric)*

⅛ yd. gold
¼ yd. tan
⅛ yd. flesh tone
⅛ yd. black
¼ yd. burgundy
½ yd. pink
⅛ yd. medium brown
⅛ yd. navy
⅛ yd. royal blue
⅛ yd. green
¼ yd. border print for crosswise cuts
    (or ¾ yd. for lengthwise cuts)

Cutting *(for outside borders)*

From the border print, cut four 3½" x 18½" strips.

Assembly

1. Sew units A–J using the Project Color Guide for color placement.

2. Make 6 each of units K and L.

3. Baste around each unit within the ¼" seam allowance and trim.

Project Assembly Diagram

(view from printed side of foundation–border not shown)

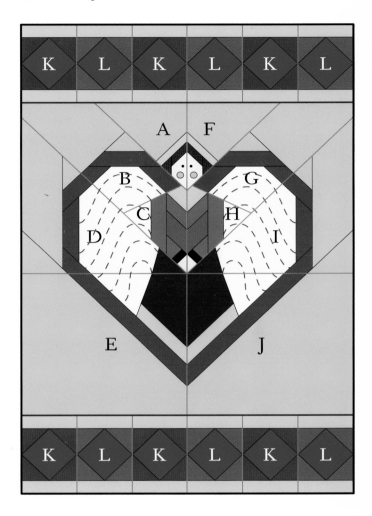

4. Arrange all the units as shown in the Project Assembly Diagram. Flip the foundations over to the fabric side and check to see if you made any errors while sewing the units.

5. Turn the foundations back to the printed side. Matching the lowercase letters in the seam allowances, sew the units together in alphabetical order.

6. Arrange the K and L units as shown in the Project Assembly Diagram or as shown in the photo on page 26. Sew the units together, then attach them to the top and bottom edges.

Project Color Guide

 - gold
- tan
- flesh tone
- black
- burgundy
- pink
- medium brown
- navy
- royal blue
- green

Border

Sew border strips to the sides first. Add the remaining strips to the top and bottom.

Finishing

1. Remove the paper from the back of the quilt top.

2. Layer the quilt top with batting and backing; baste.

3. Machine quilt the project—outline the angel and heart and stipple quilt the background.

4. Hand or machine quilt the accent lines in the angel's wings; use a metallic thread to add contrast.

5. Bind the quilt and add a hanging sleeve.

6. Sign and date your quilt.

Creative Options

Add beads for the angel's eyes, or embroider them using three strands of floss.

Use powdered blush to make the angel's cheeks pink.

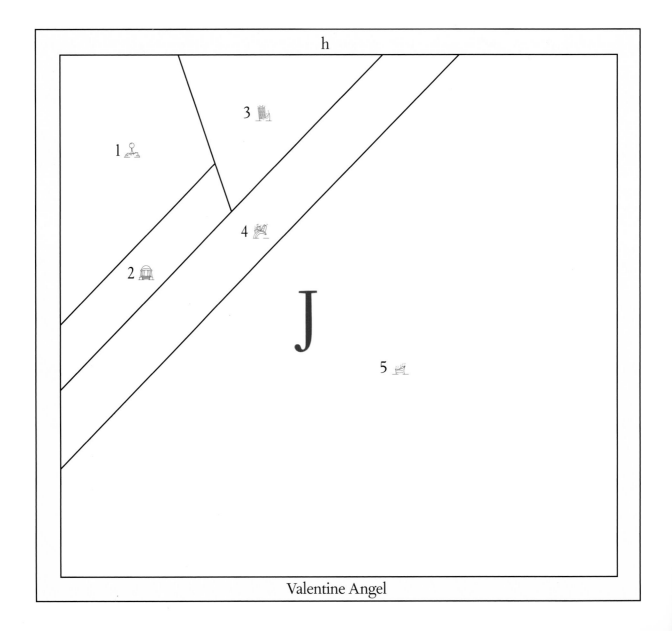

Valentine Angel

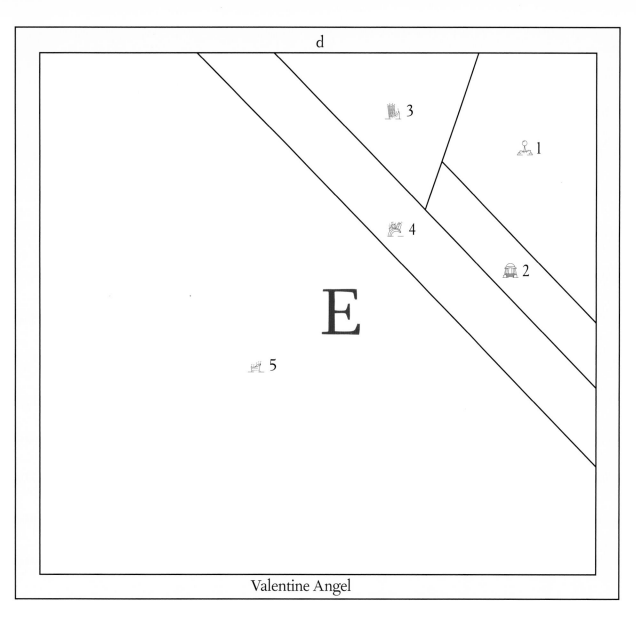

d

3

1

4

2

E

5

Valentine Angel

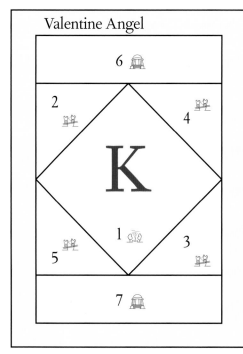

Valentine Angel

6

2

4

K

1

3

5

7

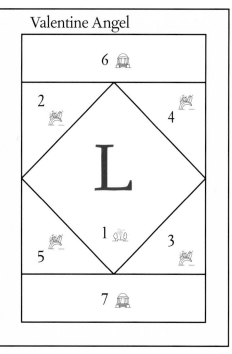

Valentine Angel

6

2

4

L

1

3

5

7

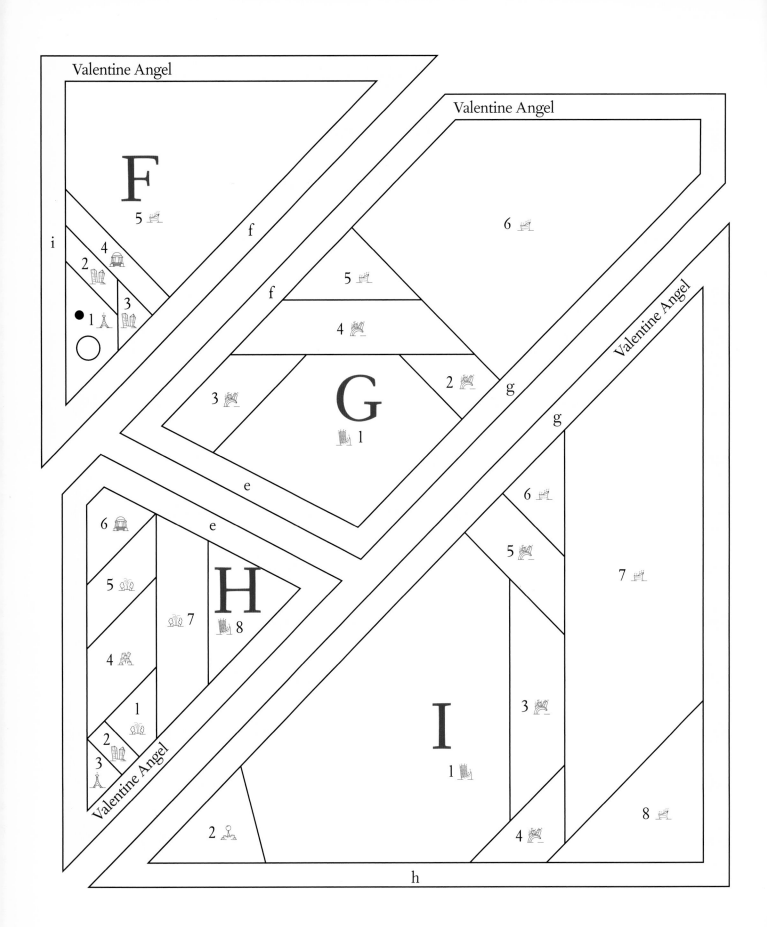

Valentine Angel

Valentine Angel

Valentine Angel

Valentine Angel

F

G

H

I

30

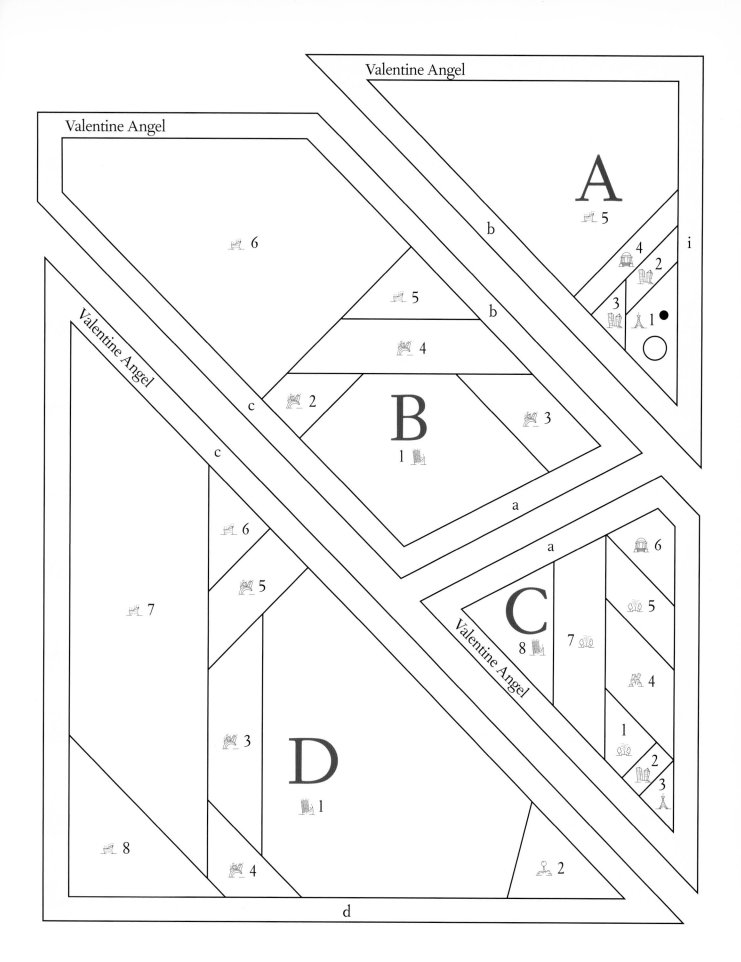

Valentine Angel

Valentine Angel

Valentine Angel

Valentine Angel

A

B

C

D

31

Country Cottage

Finished Size: 24" x 28"
Rating: Easy/Moderate

Oftentimes a country retreat affords us the space we need to unwind from our busy schedules. The fresh air and breathtaking landscape of the country transports us to a different world.

Whether we take a hike, ride a bike, or picnic in a field of wildflowers, we are sure to have time to reflect on our lives. When we are busy, we often overlook the things that are important to us. If we are in a rush, we might not see that the spring blossoms are peeking out of the earth, ready to awaken our spirits.

As you stitch up this majestic wall hanging, you will enter a world that brings peace and solitude. When you pick the colors for this project, choose fabrics that bring your dream cottage to life. Have fun with this quilt and select the colors of your blooms from the flowers that surround you.

Materials *(based on 40"-wide fabric)*

⅛ yd. sky blue
¼ yd. white
¼ yd. very dark green
¼ yd. medium dark green
½ yd. lightest dark green
¼ yd. medium green
½ yd. light green
⅛ yd. black
⅛ yd. beige
⅛ yd. dusty mauve
⅛ yd. rose
⅛ yd. pink
⅛ yd. blue
⅛ yd. medium brown
⅛ yd. yellow
⅝ yd. border print for crosswise cuts
    (or ¾ yd. for lengthwise cuts)

Cutting *(for outside borders)*

From the border print, cut two 4½" x 20½" strips and two 4½" x 24½" strips.

Assembly

1. Make one each of units A, B, D and E. Make two of unit C and 4 each of units F–J using the Project Color Guide for color placement.

Project Assembly Diagram

(view from printed side of foundation–border not shown)

2. Baste around each unit within the ¼" seam allowance and trim.

3. Arrange all the units as shown in the Project Assembly Diagram. Flip the foundations over to the fabric side and check to see if you made any errors while sewing the units.

4. Turn the foundations back to the printed side.

5. Sew sections A and B together to make the cottage, then sew a tree block (C) to each side of the house. Join sections E and D and add the unit to the top of the cottage.

6. Make the fence row by sewing the 4 section F units together; add to the bottom of the cottage.

7. To make the flowers, sew the G and H units together; repeat with the I and J sections. Alternating the flowers, sew the blocks together to make the lower flower garden. Add the row of flowers to the bottom of the quilt.

Border

Sew the long border strips to the sides of the quilt top. Add the remaining strips to the top and bottom.

Finishing

1. Remove the paper from the back of the quilt top.

2. Layer the quilt top with batting and backing; baste.

3. Machine quilt the project—outline the house, tree, and mountains; stipple quilt the background.

4. Bind the quilt and add a hanging sleeve.

5. Sign and date your quilt.

Creative Options

Embroider a wreath on the cottage door.

Add decorative buttons or brass charms to the windows or grass.

Quilt fluffy clouds in the sky.

Country Cottage

			10			
			9			
3	2	1	F / 4	5	6	7
			8			

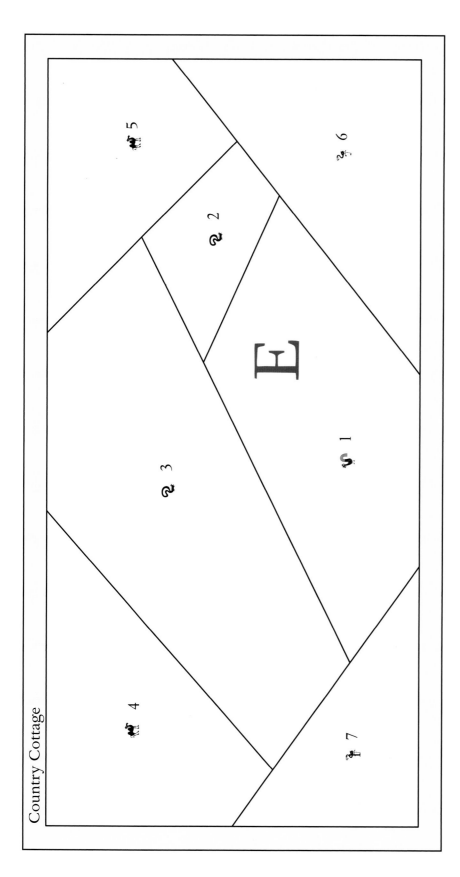

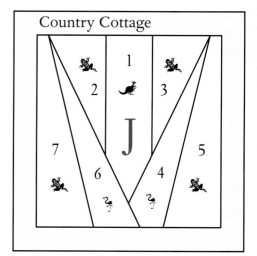

Country Cottage

Project Color Guide

- sky blue
- white
- very dark green
- medium dark green
- lightest dark green
- medium green
- light green
- black
- beige
- dusty mauve
- rose
- pink
- blue
- medium brown
- yellow

35

Country Cottage

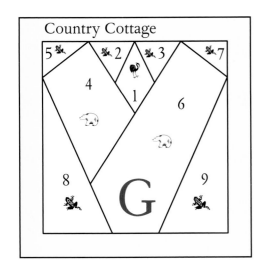

G

Country Cottage

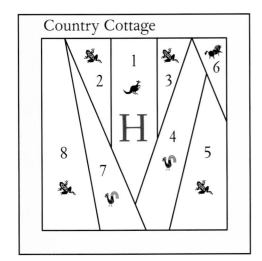

H

Country Cottage

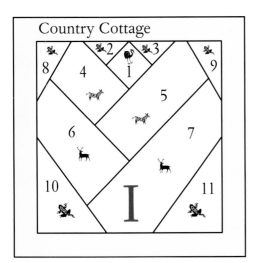

I

Country Cottage

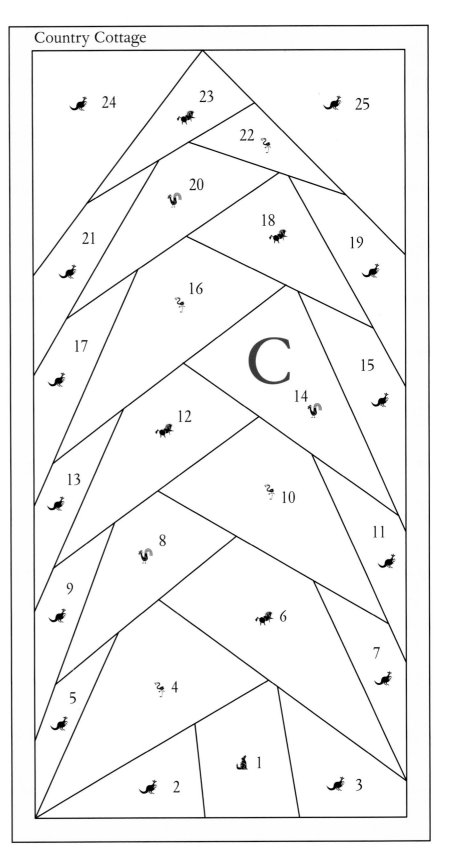

C

Country Cottage

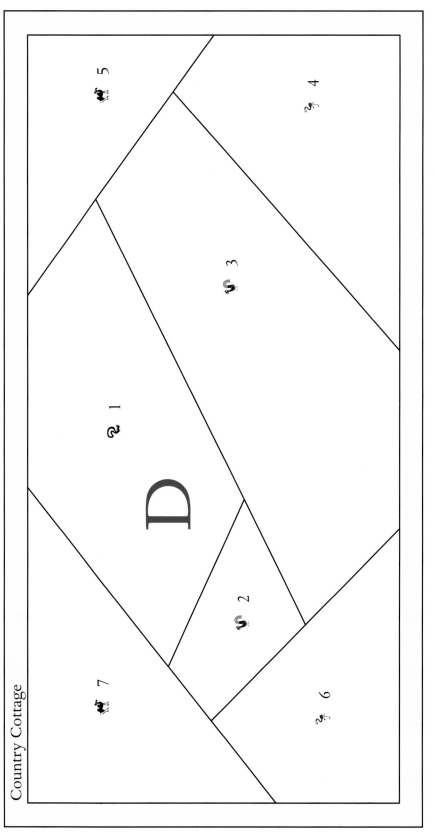

Country Cottage

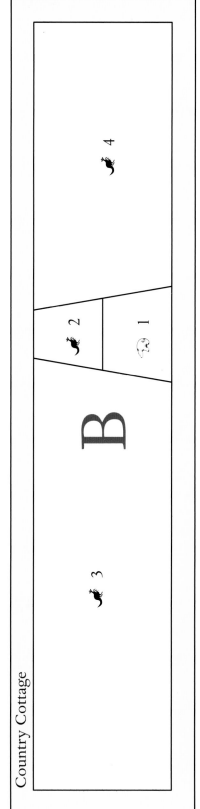

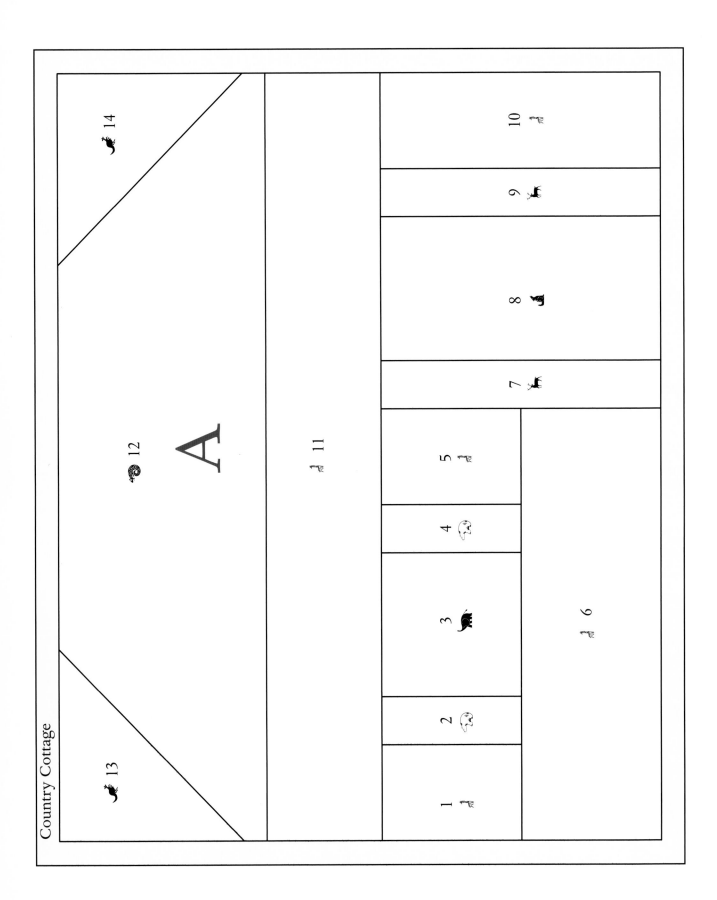

Spring

Hopping into Spring

Finished Size: 21" x 24"
Rating: Easy

As the snows of winter begin to melt and the weather turns warmer, the first signs of spring emerge. Crocus and snowdrops herald the season, and robins mske their way across tender new shoots in search of worms.

Spring is also a time for rebirth as birds feather their nests and animals introduce their young to the world. This cheerful wall hanging is a celebration of some of the icons we associate with this special time– rabbits, colorful dyed eggs, baskets, and newly hatched chicks.

Materials (based on 40"-wide fabric)
½ yd. purple
¼ yd. emerald green
¼ yd. turquoise
⅛ yd. white
⅛ yd. red
⅛ yd. pink
⅛ yd. brown
¼ yd. yellow
⅛ yd. pastel green
⅛ yd. pastel blue
⅛ yd. pastel purple
⅛ yd. pastel pink
⅛ yd. pastel yellow
¼ yd. periwinkle blue
½ yd. spring print for crosswise cuts
    (or ⅝ yd. for lengthwise cuts)

Cutting (for outside borders)
From the spring print, cut two 3½" x 18½" strips and two 3½" x 21½" strips.

Assembly
1. Sew one each of units A–F, 2 of unit K, and four each of units G–J using the Project Color Guide for color placement.

Project Assembly Diagram
(view from printed side of foundation–border not shown)

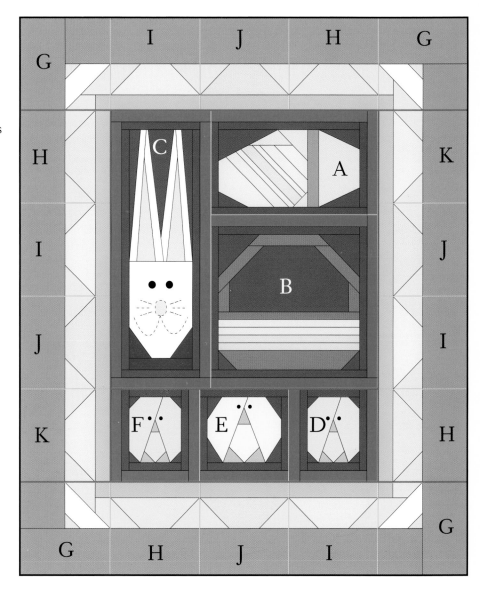

2. Baste around each unit within the ¼" seam allowance and trim.

3. Arrange units A–F as shown in the Project Assembly Diagram. Flip the foundations over to the fabric side and check to see if you made any errors while sewing the units.

4. Turn the foundations back to the printed side. Matching the lowercase letters in the seam allowances, sew the units together in alphabetical order.

5. Arrange the remaining units as shown in the Project Assembly Diagram to make the outer border. Sew the units together, then attach the short border units to the sides of the quilt top. Add the long border units to the top and bottom edges.

Border
Sew the short border strips to the sides of the quilt top. Add the remaining strips to the top and bottom.

Finishing

1. Remove the paper from the back of the quilt top.

2. Layer the quilt top with batting and backing; baste.

3. Machine quilt the project. Stipple quilt the background.

4. Embroider the bunny's face, satin stitching the nose (or use a button), and add two buttons for his eyes. Sew two small black beads to each chick to make eyes. Or, make French knots using three strands of embroidery floss.

5. Bind the quilt and add a hanging sleeve.

6. Sign and date your quilt.

Creative Options

Use a holiday print to add a treat in the basket block by centering a motif in piece 1 of unit B.

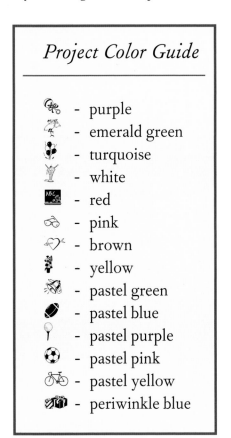

Project Color Guide

Symbol	Color
	- purple
	- emerald green
	- turquoise
	- white
ABC	- red
	- pink
	- brown
	- yellow
	- pastel green
	- pastel blue
	- pastel purple
	- pastel pink
	- pastel yellow
	- periwinkle blue

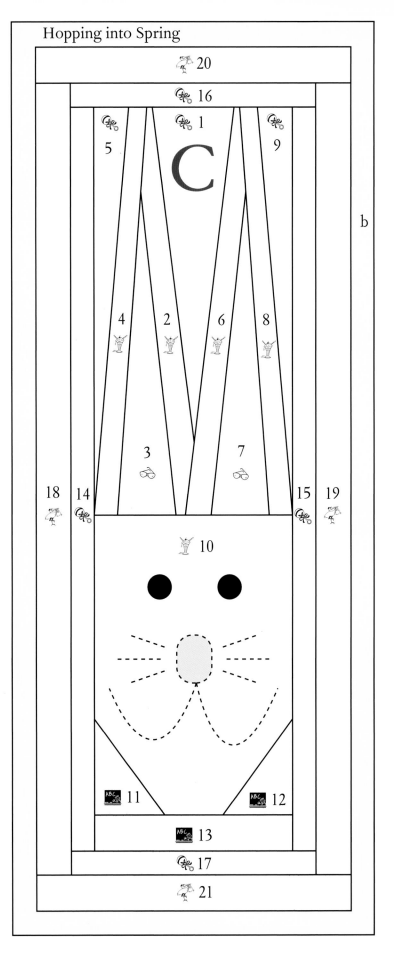

Hopping into Spring

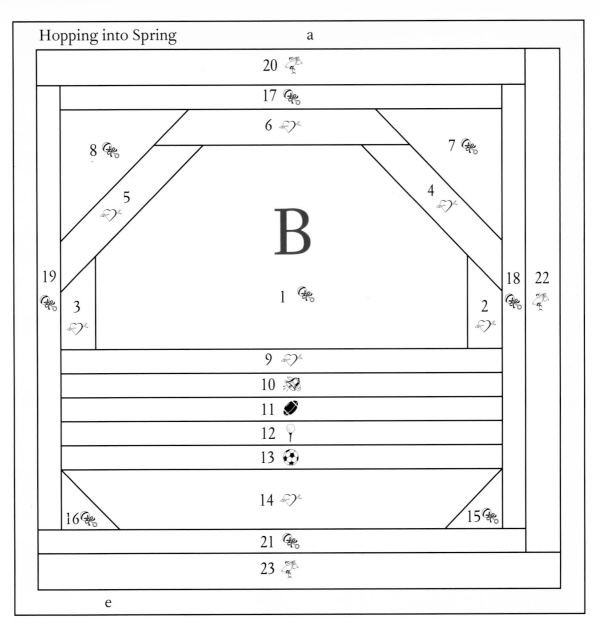

Hopping into Spring

a

20

17

6

8

7

5

4

B

19 18 22

3 1 2

9

10

11

12

13

16 14 15

21

23

e

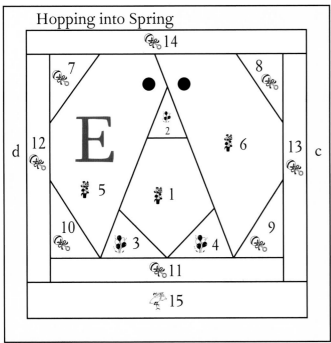

Hopping into Spring

14

7 8

E

d 12 6 13 c

5

1

10 3 4 9

11

15

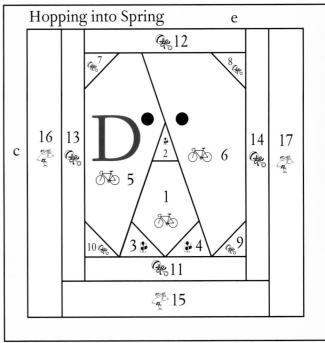

Hopping into Spring

e

12

7 8

D

c 16 13 6 14 17

5

2

1

10 3 4 9

11

15

43

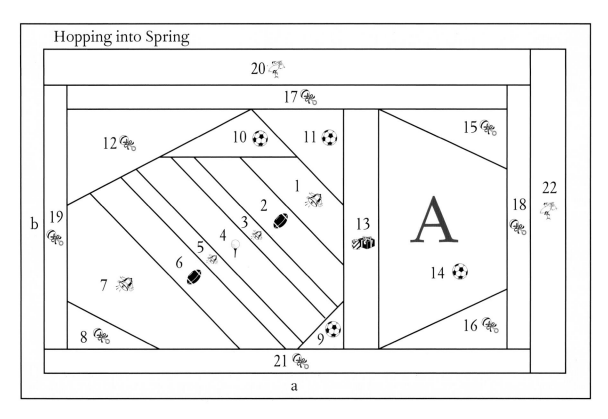

Hopping into Spring

20

17

12 10 11 15

1 22

2 19 18 b

3 13 A

4

5 14

6

7

8 9 16

21

a

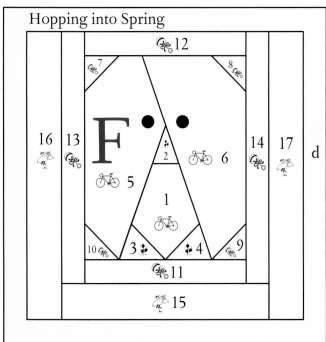

Hopping into Spring

12

7 8

16 13 F 14 17 d

2 6

5

1

10 3 4 9

11

15

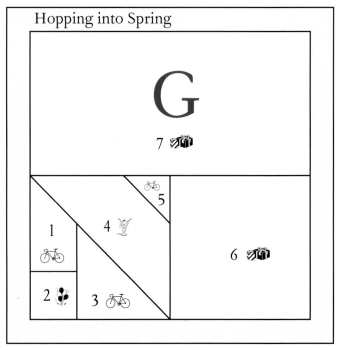

Hopping into Spring

G

7

5

1 4

6

2 3

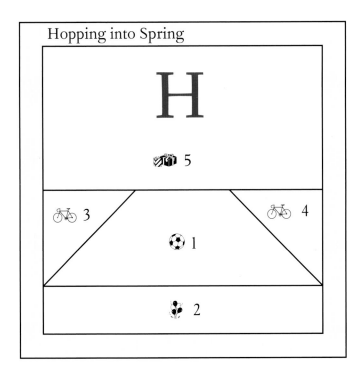

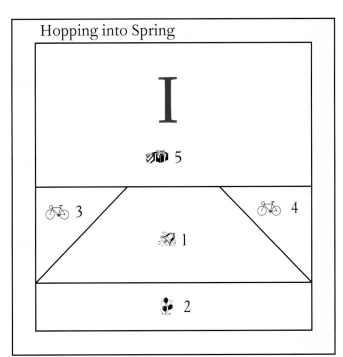

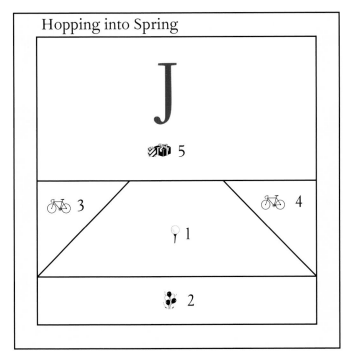

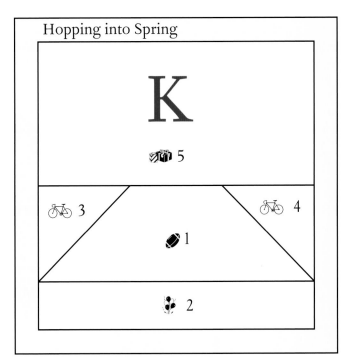

Mother's Bouquet

Finished Size: 10" x 15"
Rating: Easy

Present your mother with this everlasting bouquet of roses as a token of your appreciation for her unconditional love, kindness, and understanding over the years. This easy-to-make wall hanging is sure to bring mom pleasure all year round!

You can customize the arrangement by making the vase out of a floral fabric and using a novelty print or specialty fabric in the border.

Materials (based on 40"-wide fabric)

⅛ yd. cream
⅛ yd. light peach
⅛ yd. medium peach
⅛ yd. dark peach
⅛ yd. burnt orange
⅛ yd. green
¼ yd. leaf print
¼ yd. border print for crosswise cuts
    (or ½ yd. for lengthwise cuts)

Cutting (for outside borders)

From the border print, cut two 2½" x 6½" strips and two 2½" x 11½" strips.

Assembly

1. Make one each of units A–F and 4 of unit G using the Project Color Guide for color placement.

2. Baste around each unit within the ¼" seam allowance and trim.

3. Arrange all the units as shown in the Project Assembly Diagram. Flip the foundations over to the fabric side and check to see if you made any errors while sewing the units.

4. Turn the foundations back to the printed side. Matching the lowercase letters in the seam allowances, sew the units together in alphabetical order.

Project Assembly Diagram
(view from printed side of foundation)

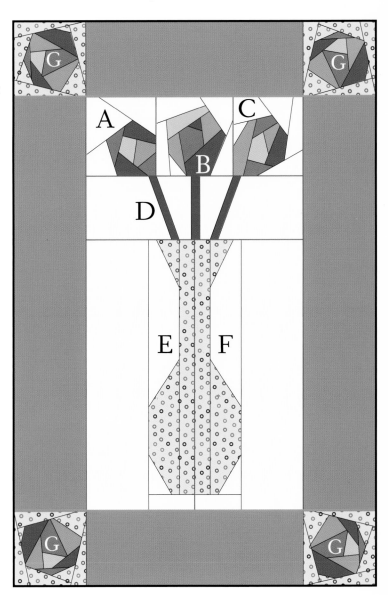

Border

1. Sew the long border strips to the sides of the quilt top.

2. Sew one G unit to each end of the remaining border strips. Add these units to the top and bottom of the quilt top.

Finishing

1. Remove the paper from the back of the quilt top.

2. Layer the quilt top with batting and backing; baste.

3. Machine quilt the project—
outline the vase and flowers. Stipple
quilt the background. If desired,
quilt a rose pattern in the border.

4. Bind the quilt and add a
hanging sleeve.

5. Sign and date your quilt.

Creative Options
Embellish the quilt with buttons,
brass charms, or silk-ribbon
embroidery.

Project Color Guide

- cream
- light peach
- medium peach
- dark peach
- burnt orange
- green
- leaf print

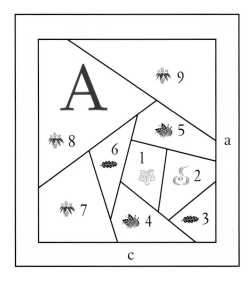

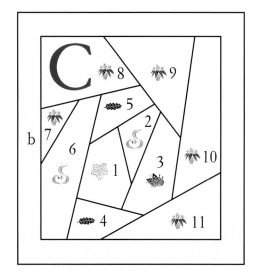

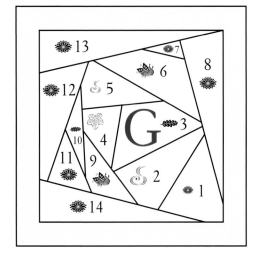

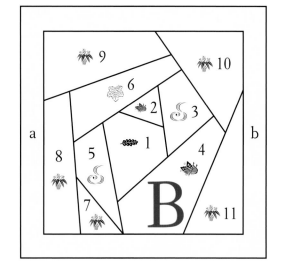

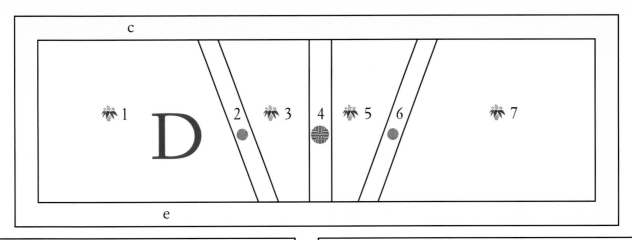

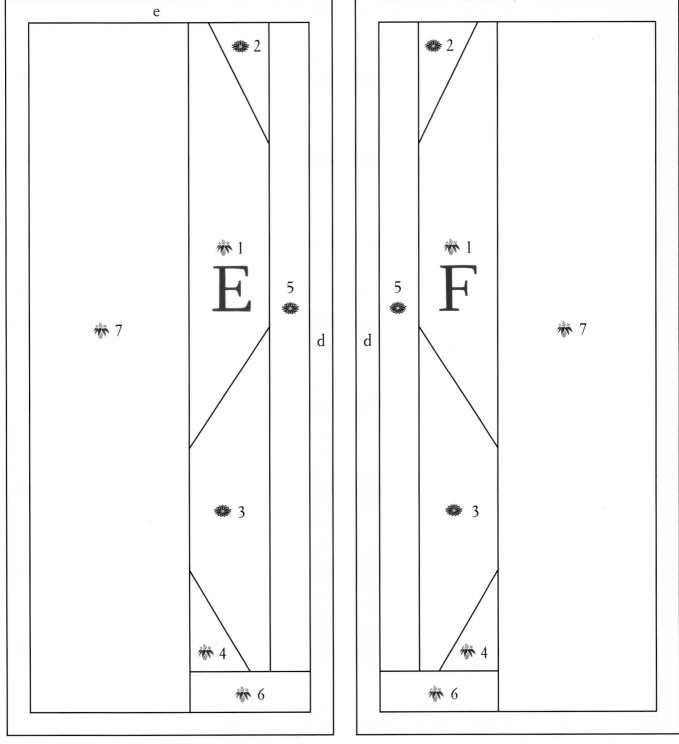

Hats Off to the Graduate

Finished Size: 21" x 21"
Rating: Easy/Moderate

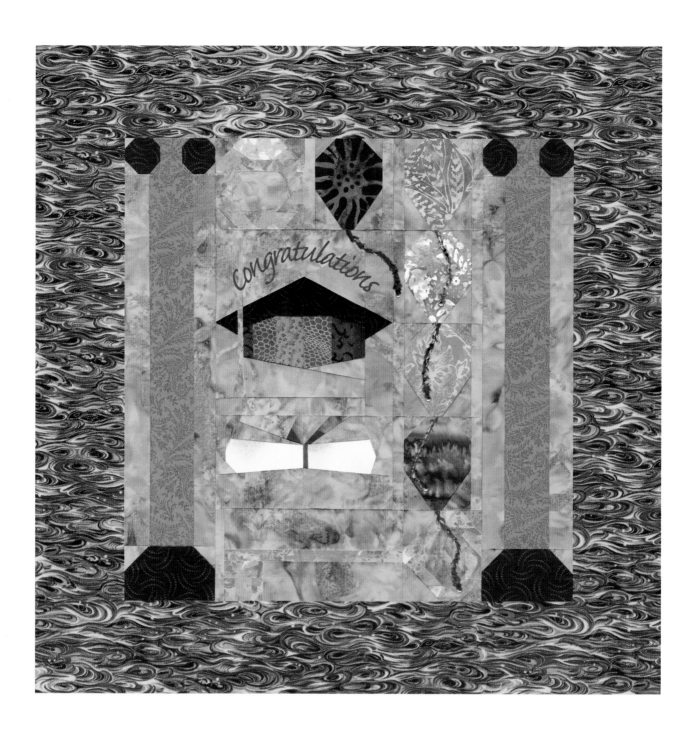

One of the most importrant milestones in our lives is the passage from academia to the outside world. Graduation initiates our transition from student to worker, and from childhood to adulthood.

Stitch up this wall hanging to celebrate the achievement of *your* special graduate. To personalize the wall hanging, use school colors in the balloons and tassel, and the make the gem in the ring the recipient's birthstone.

Materials
(based on 40"-wide fabric)
1 yd. light green
¼ yd. gold
⅛ yd. green/birthstone
⅛ yd. black
⅛ yd. dark gray
⅛ yd. medium gray
⅛ yd. light gray
⅛ yd. pale gray
⅛ yd. tan
⅛ yd. purple
⅛ yd. dark blue
¼ yd. medium blue
⅜ yd. border print for crosswise cuts (or ¾ yd. for lengthwise cuts)
One 4" x 4" square each of the following colors: turquoise, light purple, and violet

Cutting (for outside borders)
From the light green, cut four 1¼" x 12½" strips.
From the medium blue, cut two 2" x 12½" strips.
From the border print, cut two 3½" x 15½" strips and two 3½" x 21½" strips.

Project Assembly Diagram
(view from printed side of foundation—border not shown)

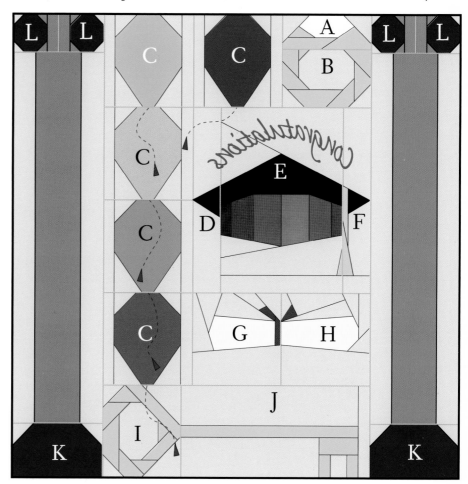

Assembly
1. Make one each of units A, B, and D–J; four of unit L; and two of unit K using the Project Color Guide for color placement.

2. Make 5 of unit C using the following colors for Piece 1: gold, dark blue, turquoise, light purple, and violet.

3. Baste around each unit within the ¼" seam allowance and trim.

4. Arrange all the units as shown in the Project Assembly Diagram. Flip the foundations over to the fabric side and check to see if you made any errors while sewing the units.

5. Turn the foundations back to the printed side.

6. Matching the lowercase letters in the seam allowances, sew the following sections together: A and B (ring); D, E, and F (graduation cap); G and H (scroll); I and J (key).

7. Arrange the light green and medium blue strips as shown in the Project Assembly Diagram, then sew them together to make the columns.

8. Join two balloon blocks along the side edges, then sew the unit to the ring (top row). Sew the graduation

cap to the scroll block. Join three balloon blocks (see Project Assembly Diagram) and attach the three-block balloon unit to the graduation cap–scroll unit (middle row).

9. Sew the L units together as shown in the Project Assembly Diagram. Add an L-L unit to the top of a column and a K unit to the bottom. Repeat to make the other column.

10. Sew the ring-balloon unit to the top of the cap-scroll-balloon unit. Add the key block to the bottom of the unit. Add the columns to the sides of the quilt top.

Border

Sew the short border strips to the sides of the quilt top. Add the remaining strips to the top and bottom.

Finishing

1. Remove the paper from the back of the quilt top.

2. Layer the quilt top with batting and backing; baste.

3. Machine quilt the project—outline the balloons, ring, hat, and scroll. Embroider the balloon tails and *Congratulations* above the cap.

4. Bind the quilt and add a hanging sleeve.

5. Sign and date your quilt.

Project Color Guide

 - light green
 - gold
 - green/birthstone
 - black
 - dark gray
 - medium gray
 - light gray
 - pale gray
 - tan
 - purple
 - dark blue
 - medium blue
 - see instructions

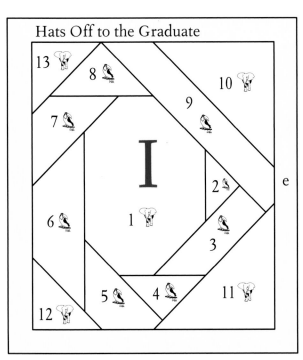

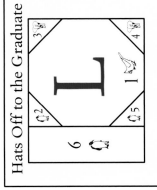

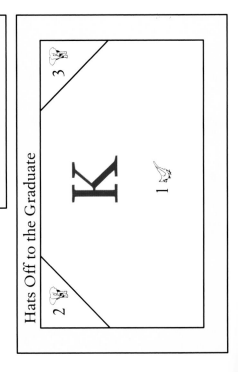

Hats Off to the Graduate

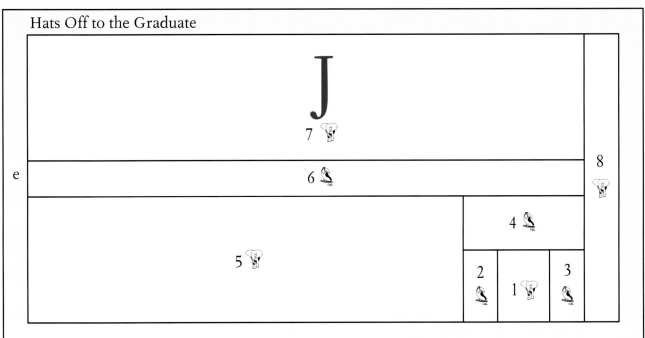

Hats Off to the Graduate

Hats Off to the Graduate

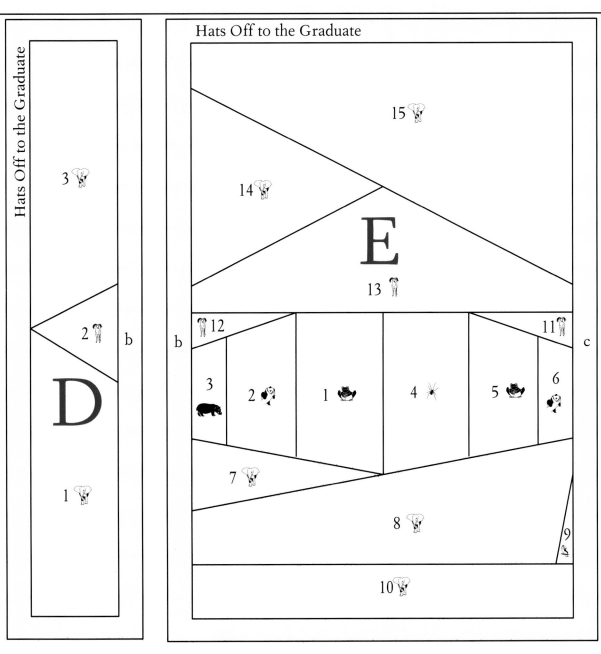

53

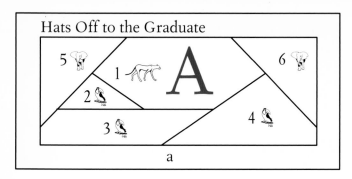

Hats Off to the Graduate

5   1   A   6
2
3

a

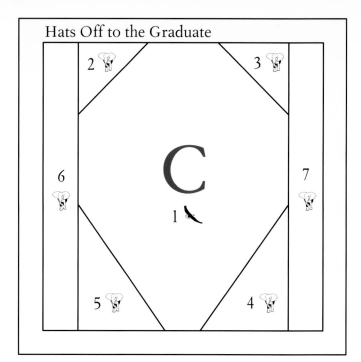

Hats Off to the Graduate

2   3

6   C   7
1

5   4

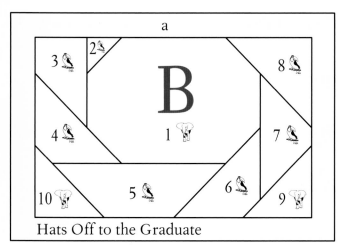

a

3   2   8

B

4   1   7

10   5   6   9

Hats Off to the Graduate

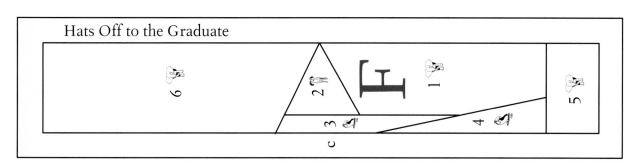

Hats Off to the Graduate

6   2   F   1   5
3   4

c

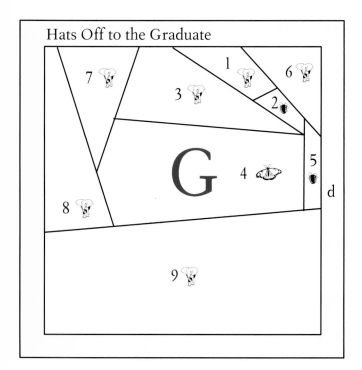

Hats Off to the Graduate

7   1   6
3   2

G   4   5

8   d

9

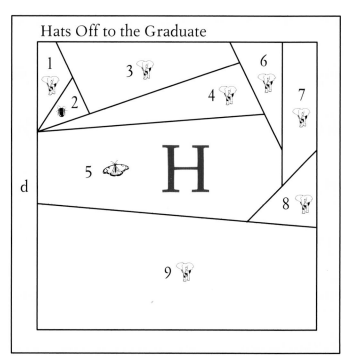

Hats Off to the Graduate

1   3   6
2   4   7

d   5   H

8

9

Summer

Patriot's Pride

Finished Size: 30" x 8"
Rating: Moderate

Throughout the world, citizens of every nation take pride in their heritage by celebrating holidays that pay tribute to the birth of their country.

In the United States, we assign symbolic meaning to the eagle (freedom), shield (patriotism), arrow (strength), and olive branch (peace). This quilt banner is one way you can decorate your home with pride.

Materials *(based on 40"-wide fabric)*

¾ yd. beige print
⅛ yd. orange
⅛ yd. yellow
⅛ yd. white
⅛ yd. black
⅛ yd. navy blue
⅛ yd. red
¼ yd. medium green
⅛ yd. dark green
⅛ yd. light brown
⅛ yd. medium brown
⅛ yd. dark brown

Assembly

1. Sew units AA–BF using the Project Color Guide for color placement.

2. Baste around each unit within the ¼ " seam allowance and trim.

3. Arrange all the units as shown in the Project Assembly Diagram. Flip the foundations over to the fabric side and check to see if you made any errors while sewing the units.

4. Turn the foundations back to the printed side. Matching the lowercase letters in the seam allowances, sew the units together in alphabetical order.

Finishing

1. Remove the paper from the back of the quilt top.

2. Layer the quilt top with batting and backing; baste.

3. Machine quilt the project–outline the eagle and stipple quilt the background.

4. Hand or machine quilt the accent lines in the eagle's wings; use a metallic thread to add contrast. Or, quilt a feather pattern in the eagle's wings.

5. Bind the quilt and add a hanging sleeve.

6. Sign and date your quilt.

Creative Options
Add three gold metallic star buttons to the top of the shield.

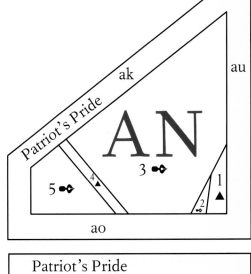

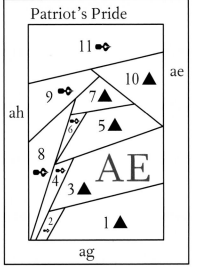

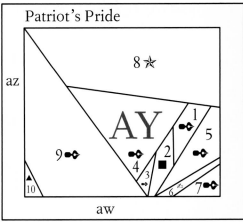

Project Assembly Diagram
(view from printed side of foundation)

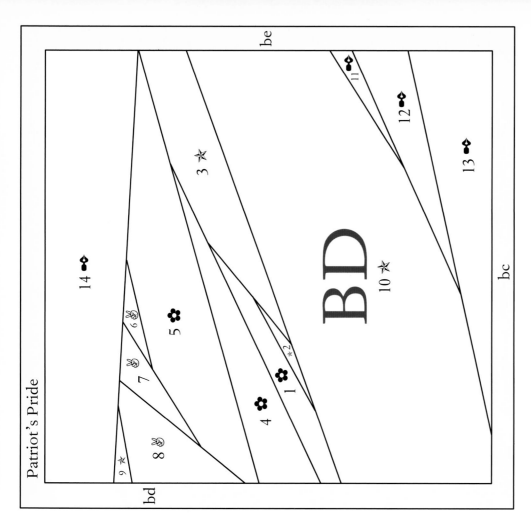

be

bc

BD

bd

Patriot's Pride

3 ☆

14 ◆

9 ✌

5 ✿

7 ✌

8 ✋

9 ☆

10 ☆

1 ✿

2 ☆

4 ✿

11

12

13 ◆

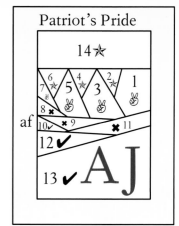

Patriot's Pride

14 ☆

7
8 ✖
6
5 ✌
4
3 ✌
2
1 ✌
10 ✔
9 ✖
11 ✖
12 ✔
13 ✔

af

AJ

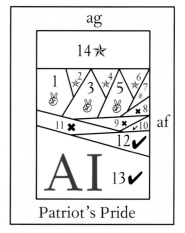

ag

14 ☆

1 ✌
2
3 ✌
4
5 ✌
6
7
8 ✖
11 ✖
9 ✖
10 ✔
12 ✔
13 ✔

af

AI

Patriot's Pride

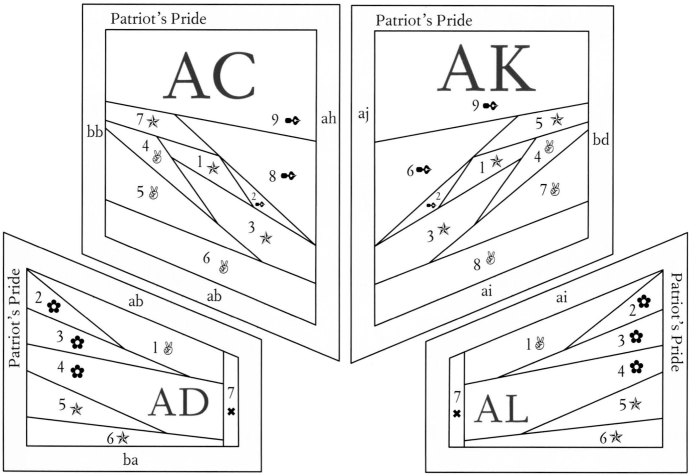

Patriot's Pride

AC

7 ☆
9 ◆
4 ✌
1 ☆
8 ◆
5 ✌
2 ◆
3 ☆
6 ✌

bb

ah

ab

ab

Patriot's Pride

2 ✿
3 ✿
4 ✿
1 ✌
5 ☆
6 ☆
7 ✖

AD

ba

Patriot's Pride

AK

9 ◆
5 ☆
6 ◆
1 ☆
4 ✌
2 ◆
3 ☆
7 ✌
8 ✌

aj

bd

ai

Patriot's Pride

2 ✿
1 ✌
3 ✿
4 ✿
7 ✖
5 ☆
6 ☆

AL

ai

58

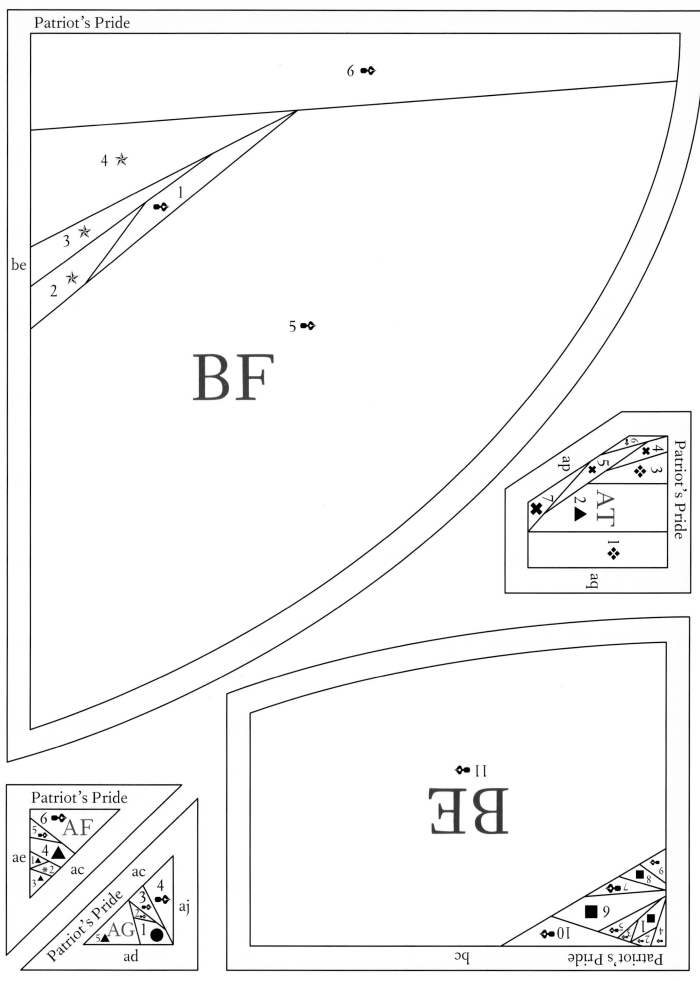

Patriot's Pride

6 ◆●

4 ✷

1

3 ✷

be

2 ✷

5 ●◆

BF

Patriot's Pride

6 ◇●
5 ✖
4 ✖
3 ❖
ap
7 ✖
2 ▶
AT
1 ❖
aq

Patriot's Pride

6 ●◆ AF
5 ◇●
ae
1 ▲ 4 ▲
✳ 2
ac
3 ▲

ac
3 ◇ 4 ●◆
2 aj
Patriot's Pride
5 ▲ AG 1 ●
ad

BE

11 ◆●

6 ◆●
8 ■
7 ◆●
9 ■
10 ◆● 5 ◆● 1 ■
4 ●◆ 2 ◆●

bc

Patriot's Pride

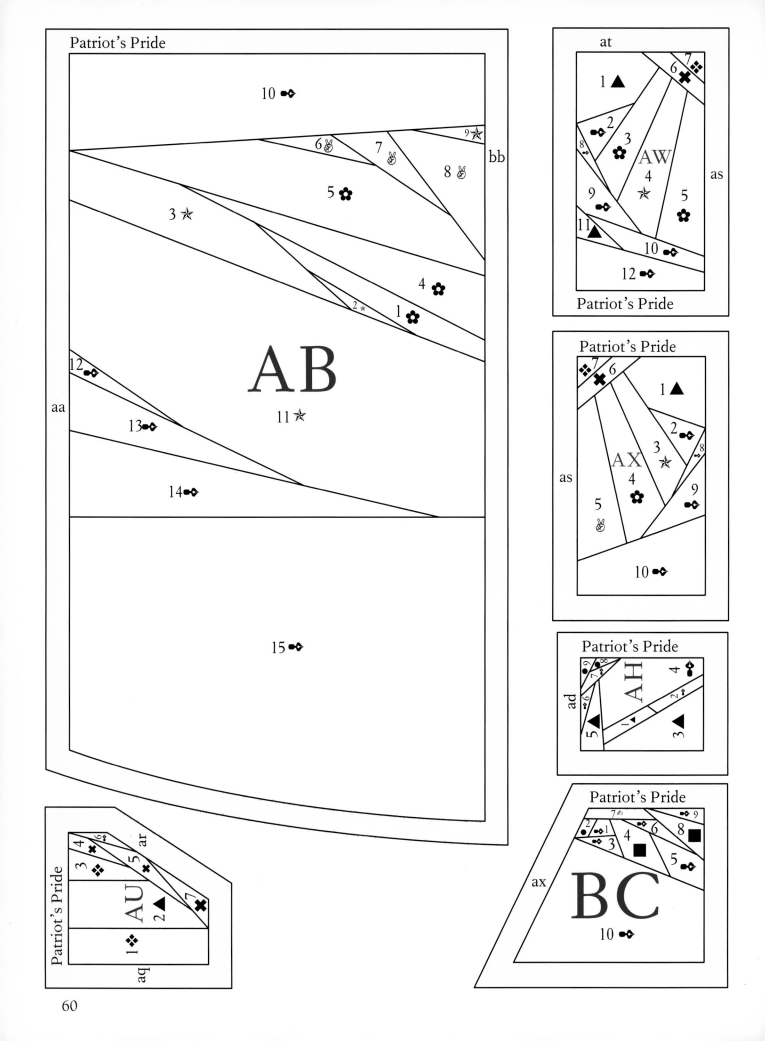

Patriot's Pride

AB

AW
as
at
Patriot's Pride

AX
as
Patriot's Pride

AH
Patriot's Pride

BC
Patriot's Pride

AU
Patriot's Pride

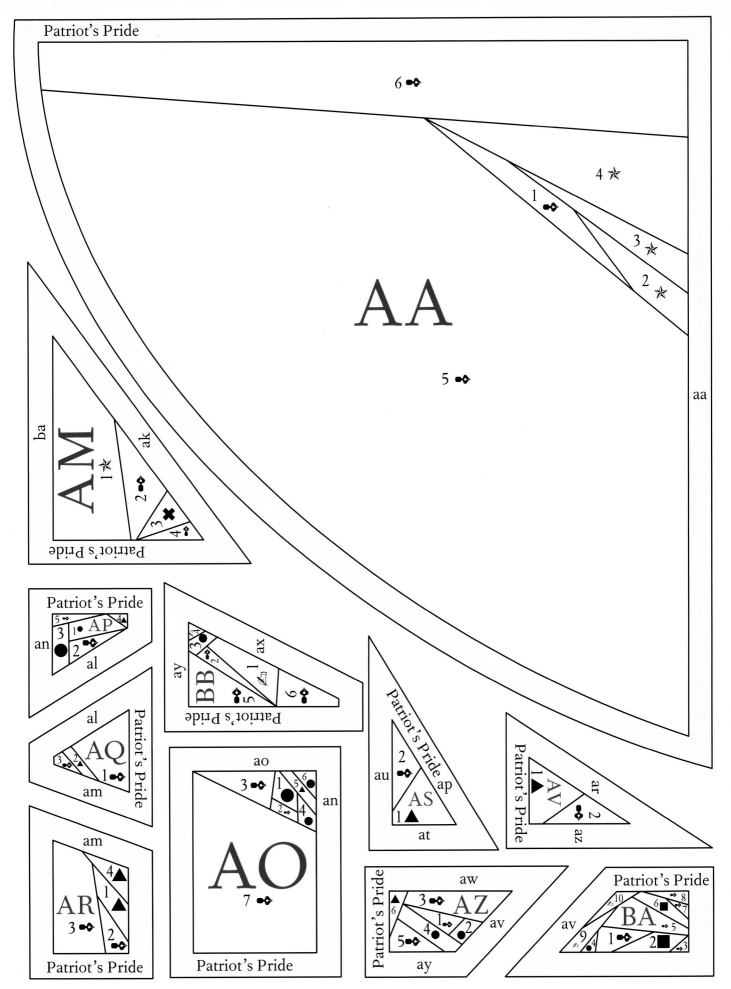

Patriot's Pride

6 ✏

4 ✦

1 ✏

3 ✦

2 ✦

AA

5 ✏

aa

ba

AM

ak

1 ✦

2 ✏

3 ✚

4 ✦

Patriot's Pride

Patriot's Pride

5 ✏   AP   4 ▲

3   1 ●

an   ●   2 ✦

al

ay

BB

3 ◆

2

1

5 ✦   6 ✦

ax

Patriot's Pride

al

AQ

3 ◆   2 ▲

1 ✏

am

Patriot's Pride

au

2 ✦

AS

ap

1 ▲

at

Patriot's Pride

AV

1 ▲

ar

2 ✦

az

am

AR

4 ▲

1 ▲

3 ✦

2 ✏

Patriot's Pride

ao

3 ✏   1 ✦   5 ▲   6

AO   2 ✦   4 ●

an

7 ✦

Patriot's Pride

Patriot's Pride

aw

▲   3 ✦   AZ

6   1 ✏   2 ●   av

4 ●   5 ✦

ay

Patriot's Pride

10   6 ■   8

7

av   BA

9   1 ✏   2 ■

4   3

61

Lookout Point

Finished Size: 24" x 24"
Rating: Moderate/Advanced

Project Assembly Diagram
(view from printed side of foundation–border not shown)

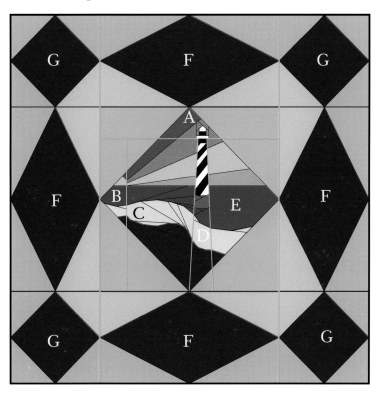

Materials (based on 40"-wide fabric)

⅛ yd. violet

⅛ yd. purple

¼ yd. amethyst

⅛ yd. magenta

⅛ yd. grass green

⅛ yd. sandy beige

¼ yd. water blue

⅛ yd. white

⅛ yd. black

¼ yd. seafoam green

⅛ yd. yellow

⅛ yd. brown

½ yd. nautical border print for crosswise cuts
   (or ¾ yd. for lengthwise cuts)

Cutting (for outside borders)
From the nautical border print, cut two 3½" x 18½"
   strips and two 3½" x 24½" strips.

Lighthouses can be found all around the world. These grand monuments continue to serve as beacons that guide sailors away from perilous coastal shoals, reefs, and rocks. Although lighthouses are buildings of utility, there is a beauty inherent in their design, which is represented in this delightful quilt. You can use a nautical print in the border to enhance the central scene.

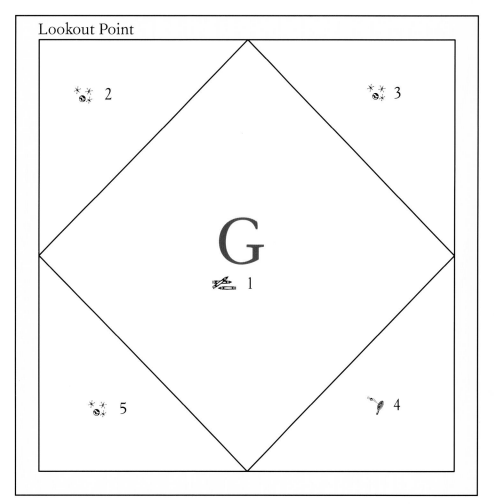

Lookout Point

Assembly

1. Make one each of units A–E, and 4 each of units F and G using the Project Color Guide for color placement.

2. Baste around each unit within the ¼" seam allowance and trim.

3. Arrange all the units as shown in the Project Assembly Diagram. Flip the foundations over to the fabric side and check to see if you made any errors sewing the units.

4. Turn the foundations back to the printed side. Matching the lowercase letters in the seam allowances, sew units A–E together in alphabetical order.

5. Sew one unit F to each side edge. Sew one unit G to each short end of the two remaining F units. Sew the pieced units to the top and bottom edges.

Border

Sew the short border strips to the sides of the quilt top. Add the remaining strips to the top and bottom.

Finishing

1. Remove the paper from the back of the quilt top.

2. Layer the quilt top with batting and backing; baste.

3. Machine quilt the project–outline the lighthouse and sky; stipple quilt the background.

4. Bind the quilt and add a hanging sleeve.

5. Sign and date your quilt.

Creative Options

Use a nautical novelty print and center the motifs in the G blocks; this will add an interesting surprise!

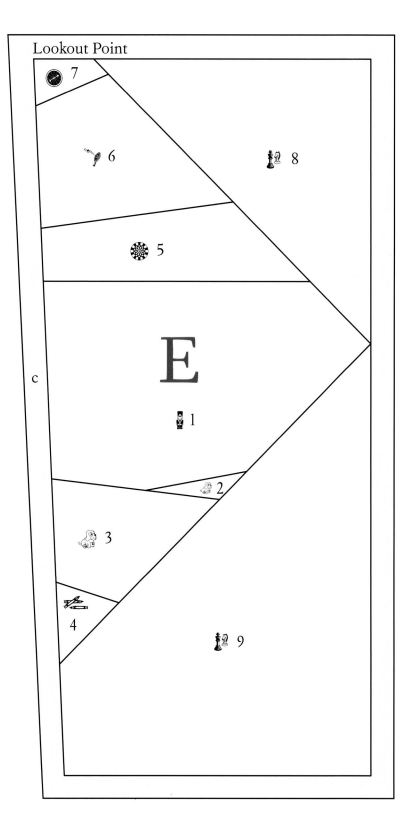

Lookout Point

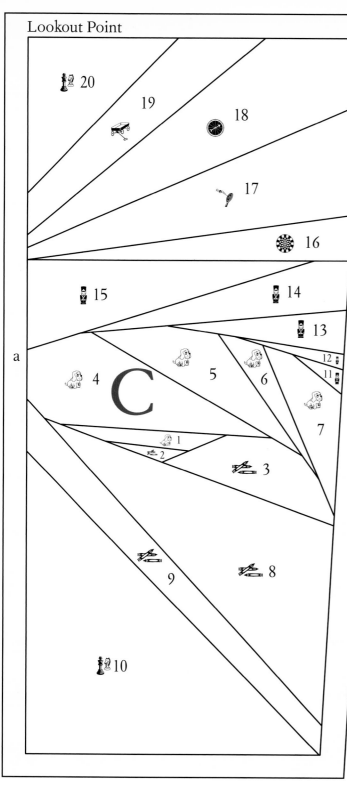
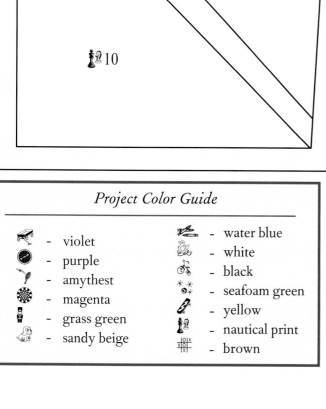
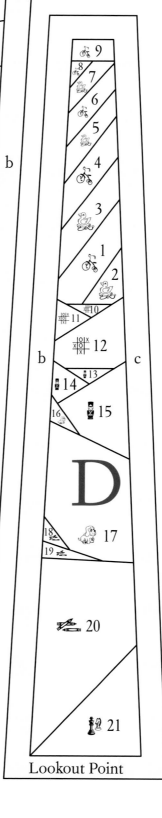
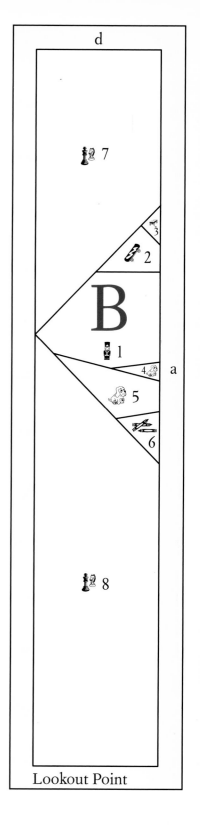

Lookout Point

20
19
18
17
16
15   14
           13
a   12 b
4   C   5   6   11
            7
        1
        2
        3
9   8
10

d

7

3
2

B
1
4   a
5
6

8

Lookout Point

9
8 7
6
5
4
3
1
2
10
11
b 12 c
13
14 15
16
D
17
18
19
20
21

Lookout Point

Project Color Guide

	– violet			– water blue
	– purple			– white
	– amythest			– black
	– magenta			– seafoam green
	– grass green			– yellow
	– sandy beige			– nautical print
				– brown

65

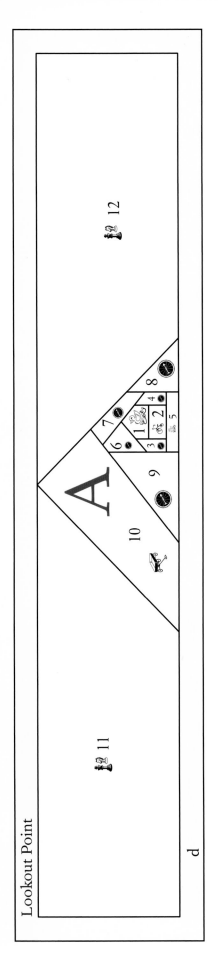

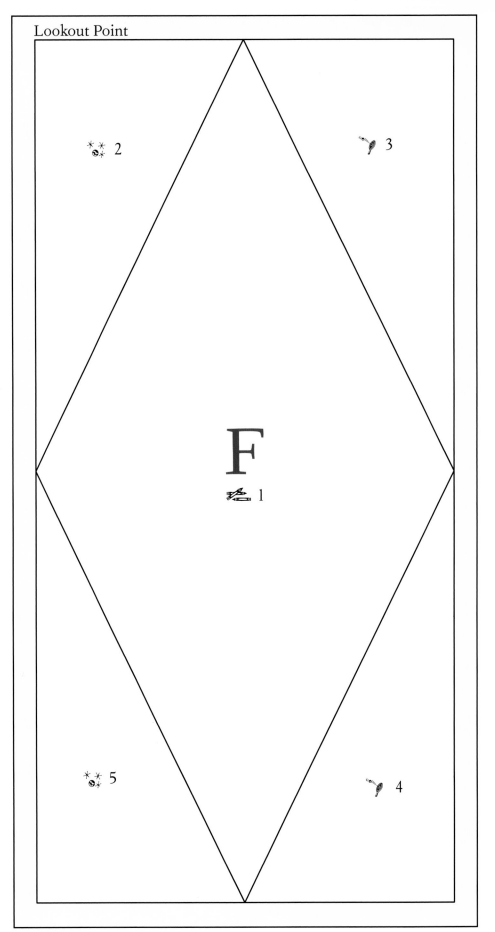

Apple Banner

Finished Size: 30" x 14"
Rating: Easy/Moderate

Who can resist the smell of a freshly baked apple pie as it comes out of the oven? Making apple pie is a revered American tradition.

This charming apple wall hanging is a quick and easy gift to make, and it can easily be stitched up in a weekend.

Materials *(based on 40"-wide fabric)*

½ yd. slate blue

⅛ yd. light green

⅛ yd. medium green

⅛ yd. dark green

⅛ yd. gold

⅛ yd. brown

¼ yd. apple print for crosswise cuts
    (or ¾ yd. for lengthwise cuts)

⅛ yd. burgundy for crosswise cuts
    (or ⅞ yd. for lengthwise cuts)

¼ yd. green plaid for crosswise cuts
    (or ⅞ yd. for lengthwise cuts)

Cutting *(for outside borders)*

From the apple print, cut two 2½" x 6½" strips, two
    2½" x 10½" strips, and two 2½" x 22½" strips.

From the burgundy, cut two 1" x 11½" strips and two
    1" x 26½" strips.

From the green plaid, cut two 2" x 14½" strips and
    two 2" x 27½" strips.

Assembly

1. Make one each of apple units 1–3 using the Project Color Guide for color placement.

2. Baste each unit within the ¼" seam allowance and trim.

3. Arrange all the units as shown in the Project Assembly Diagram. Flip the foundations over to the fabric side and check to see if you made any errors while sewing the units.

4. Turn the foundations back to the printed side. Matching the lowercase letters in the seam allowances, sew the units together in alphabetical order.

5. Sew one 2½" x 6½" strip of the apple print to each side of the middle apple. Add the remaining blocks to each side.

Borders

Starting with the apple print, sew the long strips to the top and bottom of the quilt top. Add the remaining strips to the sides. Sew the burgundy border and green plaid border to the quilt in the same way.

Finishing

1. Remove the paper from the back of the quilt top.

2. Layer the quilt top with batting and backing; baste.

3. Machine quilt the project—outline the apples; if desired, quilt an apple motif in the green plaid border.

4. Bind the quilt and add a hanging sleeve.

5. Sign and date your quilt.

Project Color Guide

- ✳ - slate blue
- ⊕ - light green
- ✛ - medium green
- ✳ - dark green
- ▦ - gold
- ✸ - brown
- ◉ - burgundy

Project Assembly Diagram
(view from printed side of foundation)

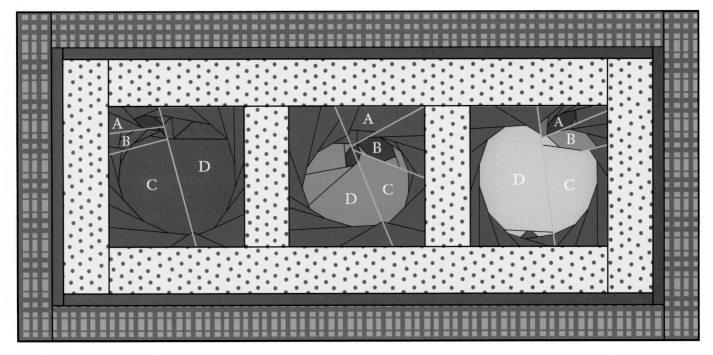

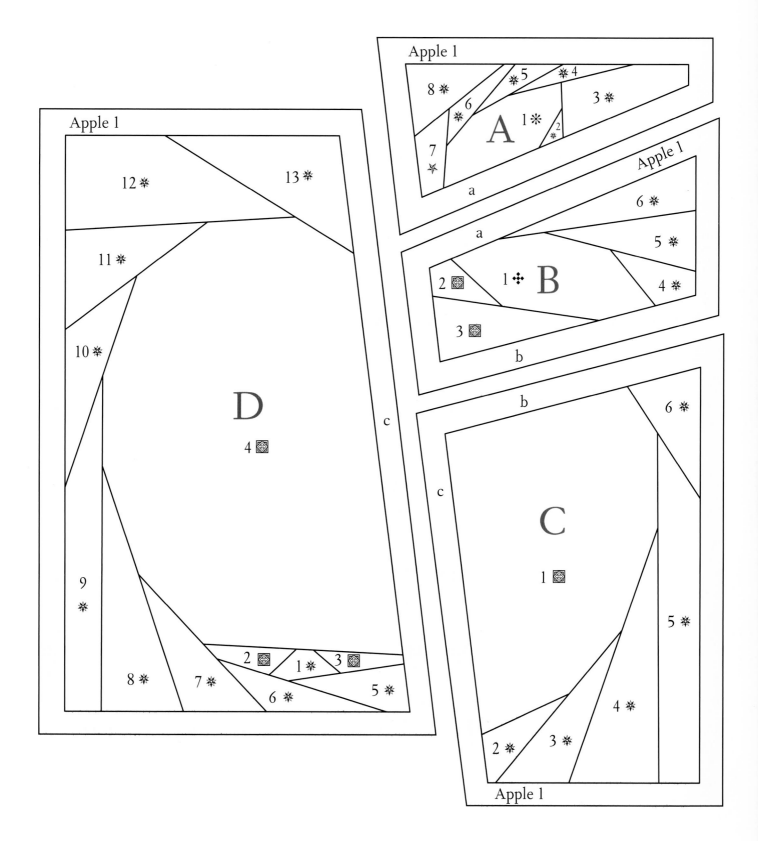

69

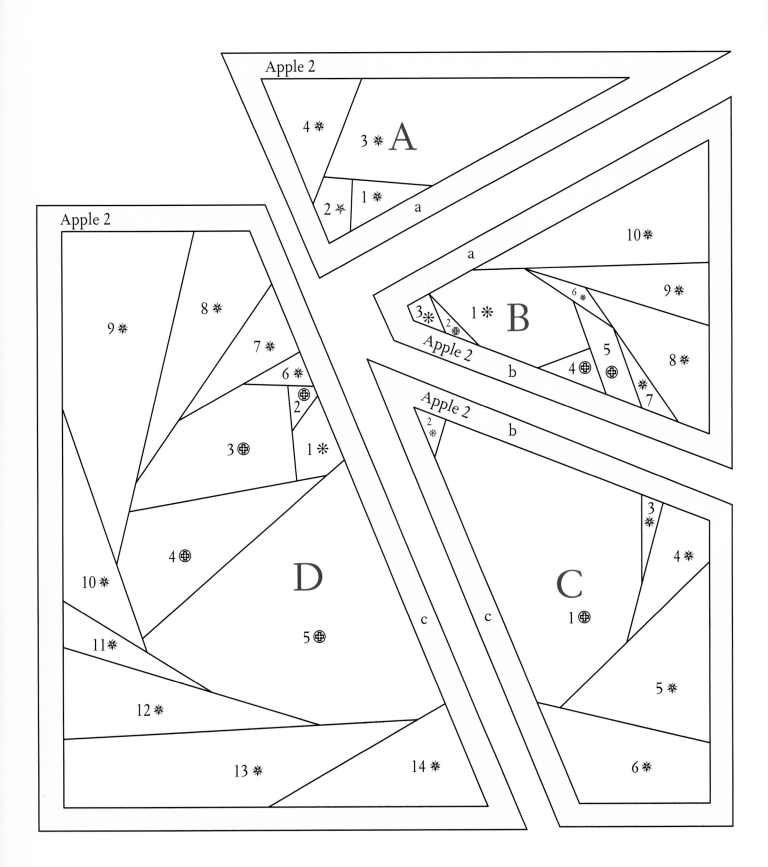

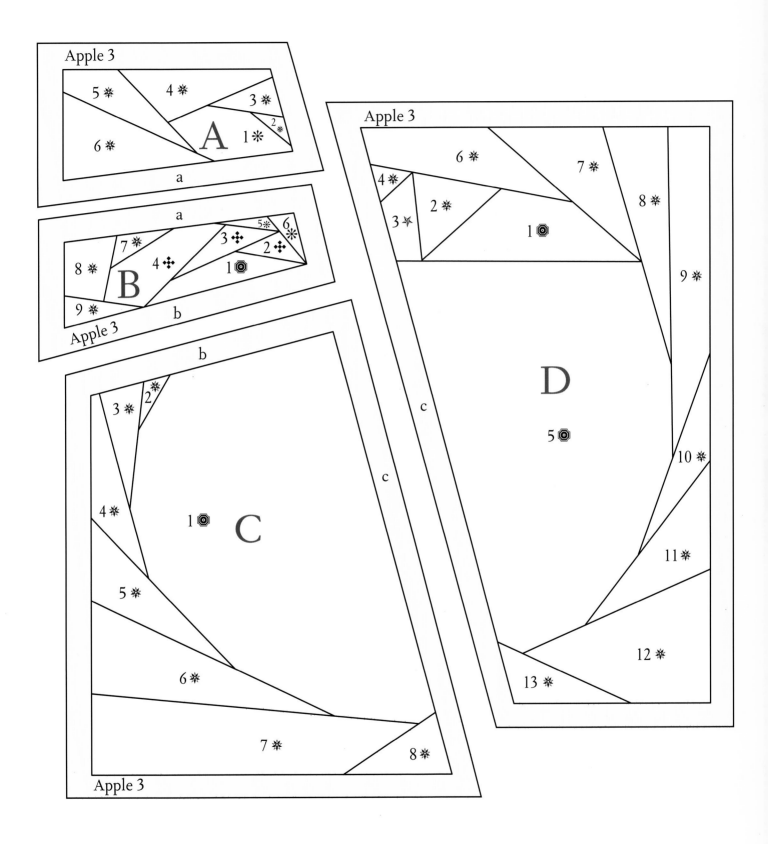

71

Fall

Country Road

Finished Size: 26" x 22"
Rating: Advanced

Covered bridges are a link to the past, reminding us of simpler, more genteel times. The creaking of floorboards makes us think of how our foremothers and fathers spent their days and what adventures they had.

This wall hanging captures the beauty of a special place as fall comes to a close and winter draws near. An oval frame creates a nostalgic mood in this lovely portrait.

Materials *(based on 40"-wide fabric)*
⅛ yd. sky blue
¼ yd. water blue
⅛ yd. beige (stones)
⅛ yd. brown (stones)
⅛ yd. dark green
⅛ yd. medium green
⅛ yd. light green
⅛ yd. dark gray (gravel)
½ yd. dark blue-green
¾ yd. medium blue-green
⅛ yd. burnt orange
⅛ yd. silver
⅛ yd. dark brown
⅛ yd. medium brown
⅛ yd. light brown
⅛ yd. black
⅛ yd. white
⅛ yd. burgundy
⅛ yd. scarlet
⅛ yd. gold
½ yd. leaf print for crosswise cuts
   (or ¾ yd. for lengthwise cuts)

Cutting *(for outside border)*
From the leaf print, cut two 3½" x 16½" strips and two 3½" x 26½" strips.

Assembly
1. Sew units A–R using the Foundation Color Guide for color placement.

2. Baste around each unit within the ¼" seam allowance and trim.

3. Arrange all the units as shown in the Quilt Assembly Diagram. Flip the foundations over to the fabric side and check to see if you made any errors while sewing the units.

Project Color Guide

A - sky blue
B - water blue
C - beige (stones)
D - brown (stones)
E - dark green
F - medium green
G - light green
H - dark gray (gravel)
I - dark blue-green
J - medium blue-green
K - burnt orange
L - silver
M - dark brown
N - medium brown
O - light brown
P - black
Q - white
R - burgundy
S - scarlet
T - gold

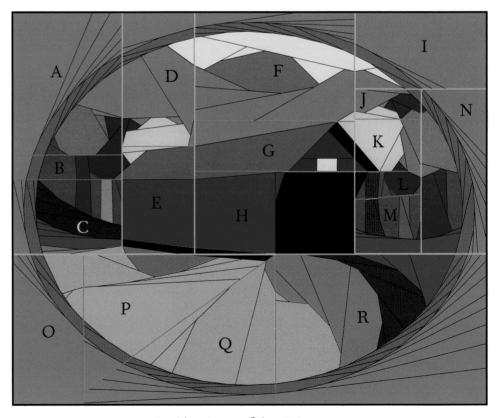

Quilt Assembly Diagram
(view from printed side of foundation–border not shown)

4. Turn the foundations back to the printed side. Matching the lowercase letters in the seam allowances, sew the units together in alphabetical order.

Borders

Sew the short border strips to the sides of the quilt top. Add the remaining strips to the top and bottom.

Finishing

1. Remove the paper from the back of the quilt top.

2. Layer the quilt top with batting and backing; baste.

3. Machine quilt the project as desired.

4. Bind the quilt and add a hanging sleeve.

5. Sign and date your quilt.

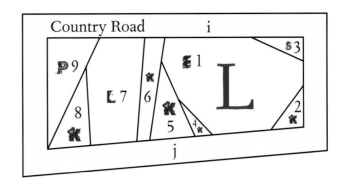

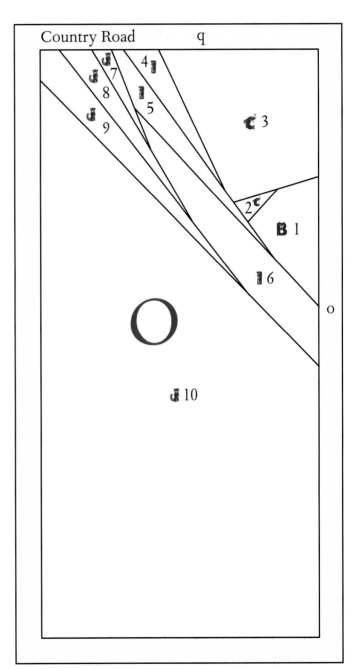

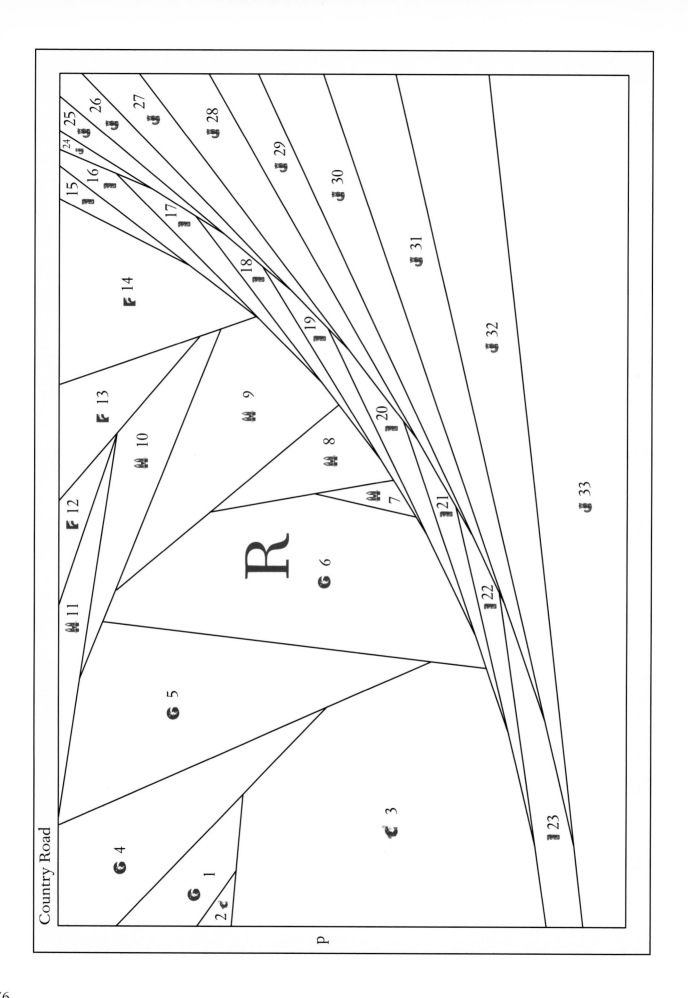

Country Road

P

76

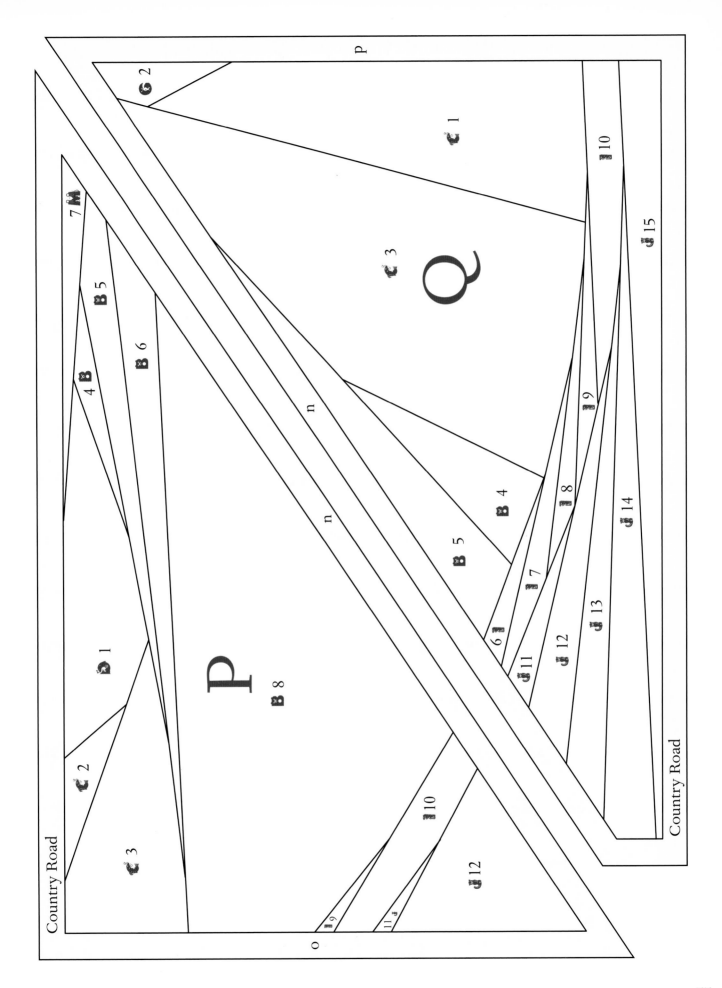

77

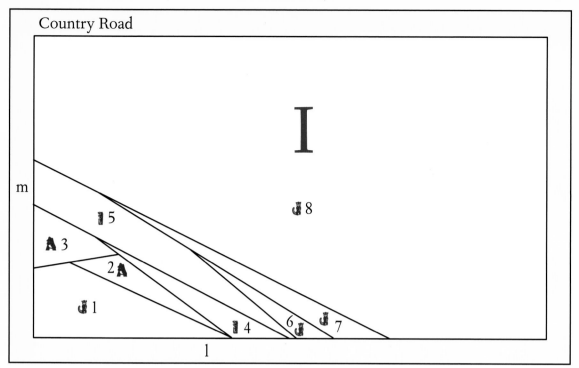

Country Road

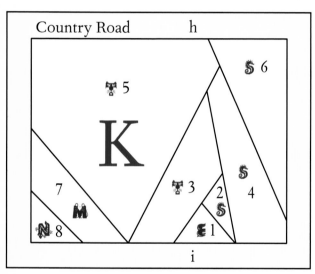

Country Road

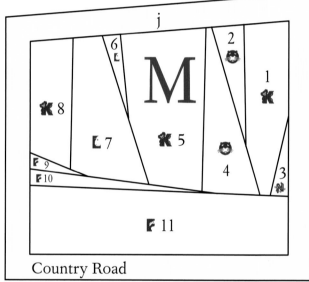

Country Road

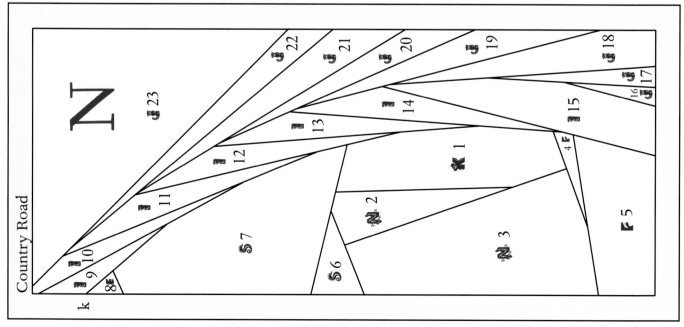

Country Road

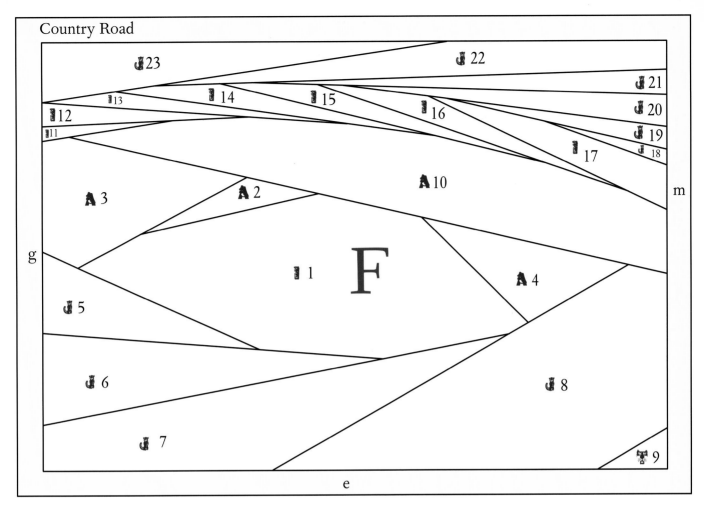

Country Road

J23   J22

I13   I14   I15   J21

I12   I16   J20

I11   J19
J18

I17   m

A3   A2   A10

g

I1   F   A4

J5

J6   J8

J7   T9

e

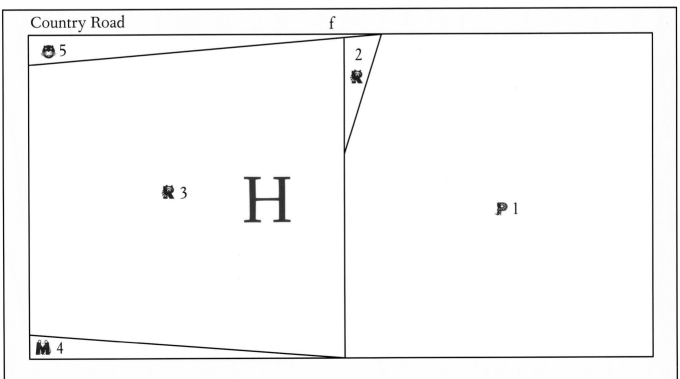

Country Road   f

5   2

R

P1

R3   H

M4

C

Country Road — b

22 21 19 18 7 1
8 2
K 3
9 L 4
6 R
K 5

11
12
13
10

23 20 14
15
16 17

q

J

Country Road

k
10
6 5
9 1
l 4
2
7 3
J
8
h

D

Country Road

15
13
14 A 10
12
11
D
g
8
7
d
6 2 3 4
1 5
9
c

E

Country Road — c

4
1
2 3
E
5
6
7 8

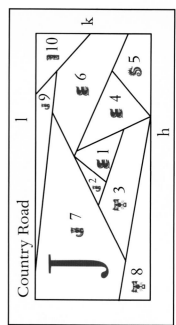
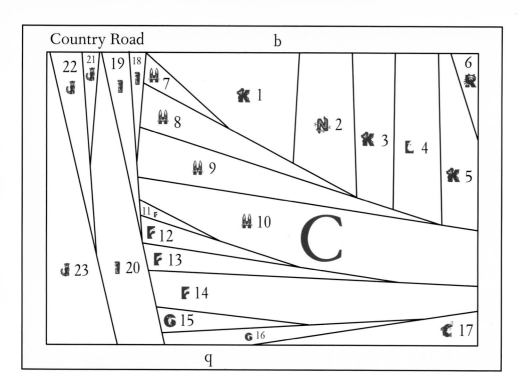
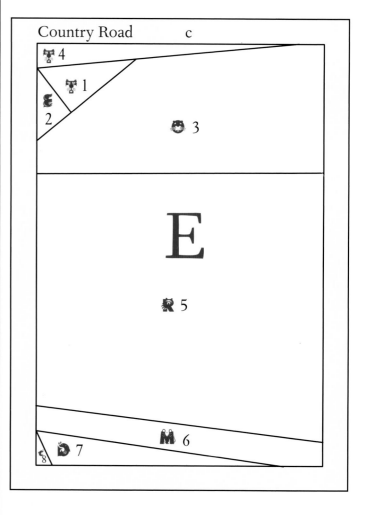
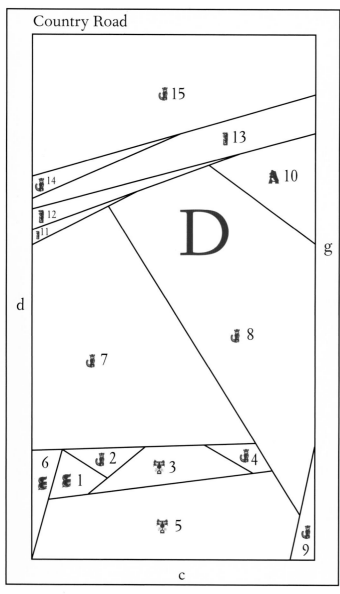

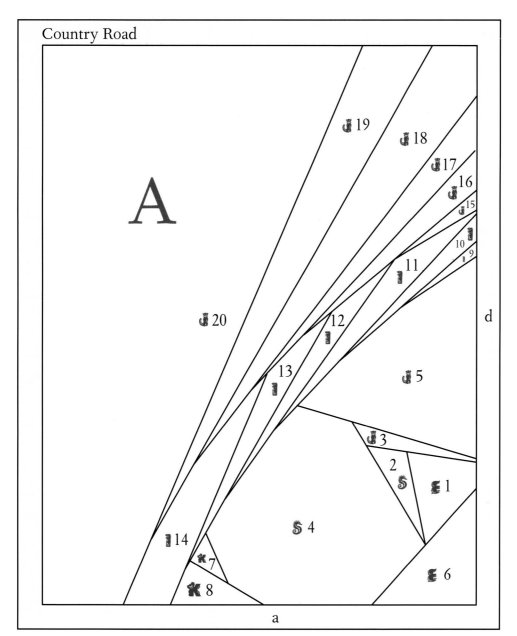

Country Road

A

🜚19 🜚18 🜚17 🜚16 15 🜚
🜚20 📜11 10 9
12
13 🜚5
🜚3
2 §
🍀1
§4 🍀6
📜14
🦋7
🦋8
d
a

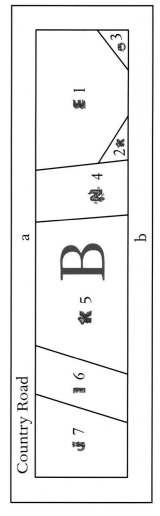

B

🜚7 / 📜6 🦋5
📜1 🦋2 🌿4 🍀3
a
b
Country Road

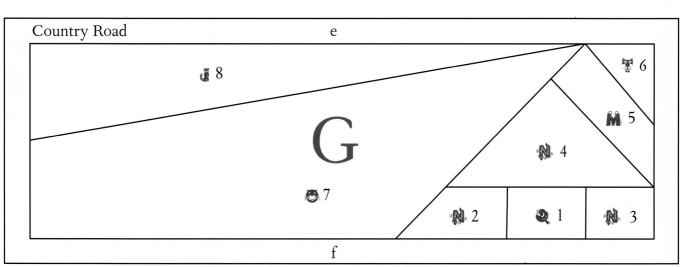

Country Road   e

🜚8

G

🪲7

🦋6
🅼5
🌿4
🌿2 🍀1 🌿3

f

Fruits of Our Labour

Finished Size: 26" x 22"
Rating: Advanced/Challenging

Quilters are inspired by the rich tapestry of colors and textures that surround them. Often, ideas for quilts come from important events in our lives. This quilt portrays the bounty of the fall harvest and and includes all of the brilliant colors of the season.

Materials (based on 40"-wide fabric)

¾ yd. cream
¼ yd. dark brown
¼ yd. medium brown
½ yd. light brown
¼ yd. taupe
⅛ yd. very dark orange
⅛ yd. dark orange
⅛ yd. medium orange
⅛ yd. light orange
⅛ yd. hunter green
⅛ yd. dark green
⅛ yd. medium green
⅛ yd. medium-light green
⅛ yd. medium yellow
⅛ yd. light yellow
⅛ yd. dark red
⅛ yd. medium red
⅛ yd. plum
⅛ yd. grape
⅛ yd. violet
⅛ yd. purple
⅛ yd. magenta
⅛ yd. white
½ yd. border print for crosswise cuts
　　(or ¾ yd. for lengthwise cuts)

Cutting (for outside borders)

From the border print, cut
　　two 3½" x 20½" strips and
　　two 3½" x 22½" strips.

Quilt Assembly Diagram
(view from printed side of foundation—border not shown)

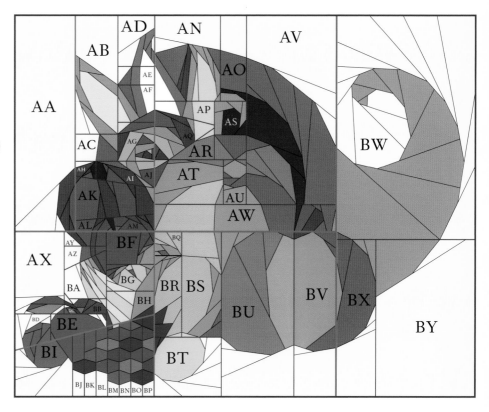

Assembly

1. Sew units AA–BY using the Foundation Color Guide for color placement.

2. Baste around each unit within the ¼" seam allowance and trim.

3. Arrange all the units as shown in the Quilt Assembly Diagram. Flip the foundations over to the fabric side and check to see if you made any errors while sewing the units.

4. Turn the foundations back to the printed side. Matching the lowercase letters in the seam allowances, sew the units together in alphabetical order.

Borders

Sew the short border strips to the top and bottom of the quilt top. Add the remaining strips to the sides.

Finishing

1. Remove the paper from the back of the quilt top.

2. Layer the quilt top with batting and backing; baste.

3. Machine quilt the project, outlining the fruits and vegetables—you can add dimensional accents to the fruits by quilting curved lines to echo the seam lines.

4. Bind the quilt and add a hanging sleeve.

5. Sign and date your quilt.

Project Color Guide

- ♡ – cream
- – dark brown
- – medium brown
- – light brown
- – taupe
- – very dark orange
- – dark orange
- – medium orange
- – light orange
- – hunter green
- – dark green
- – medium green

- – medium-light green
- – medium yellow
- – light yellow
- – dark red
- – medium red
- – plum
- – grape
- – violet
- – purple
- – magenta
- – white

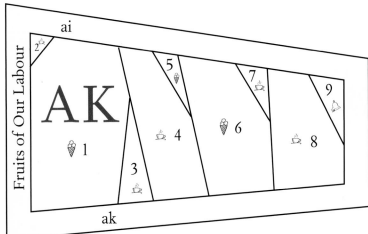

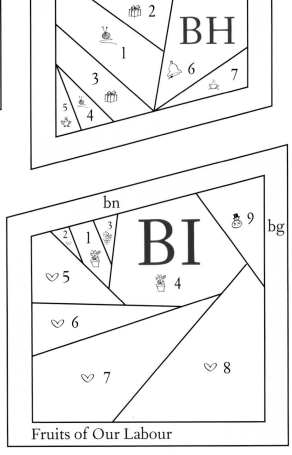

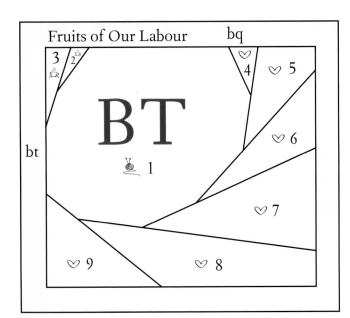

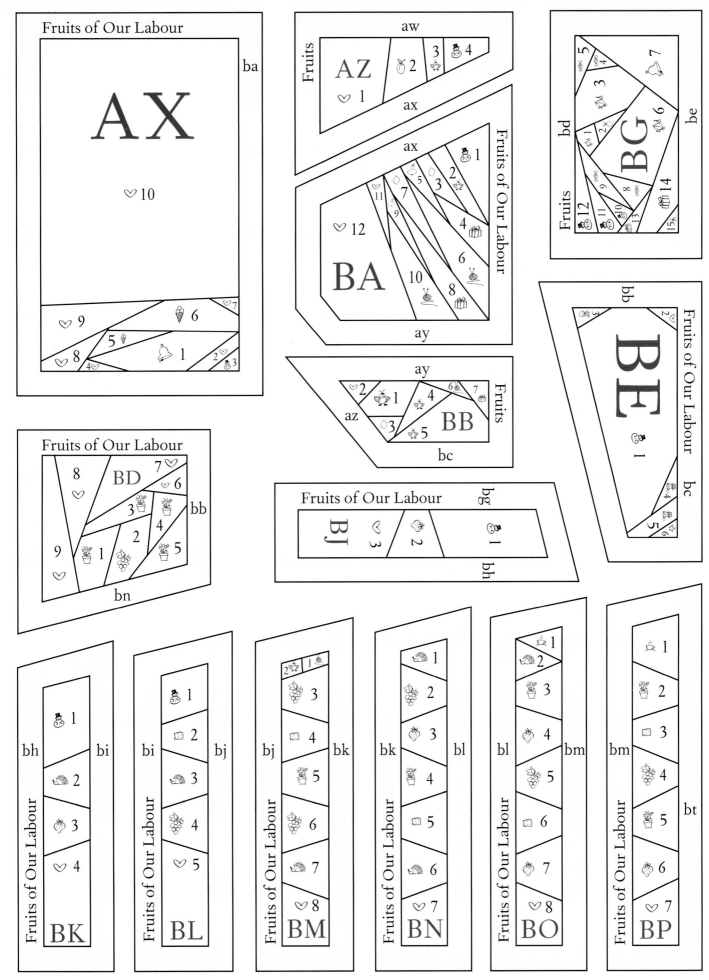

Fruits of Our Labour

85

Fruits of Our Labour

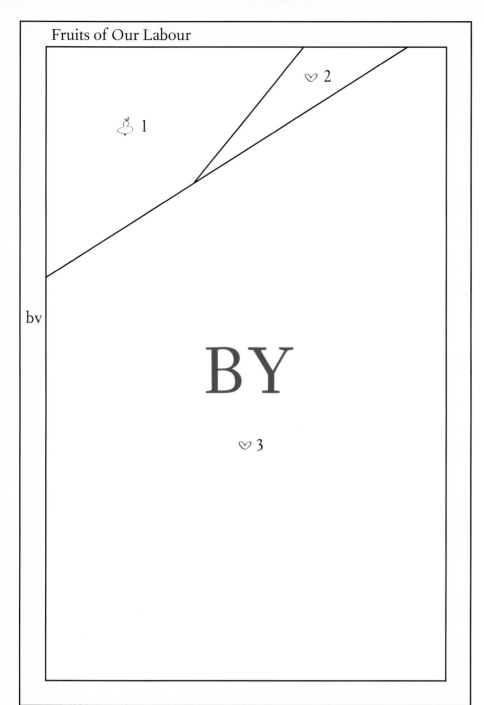

🔔 1

♡ 2

bv

BY

♡ 3

Fruits

bw

🍒 1

🍐 4

🍐 5

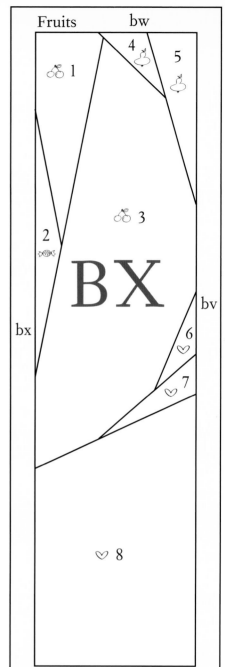

🍒 3

2
🍬

bx

BX

bv

♡ 6

♡ 7

♡ 8

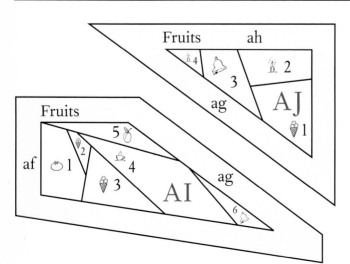

Fruits

ah

🍐 4

🔔 3

🕯 2

ag

AJ

🍦 1

Fruits

af

🍅 1

🍐 2

🍐 5

☕ 4

🍦 3

ag

AI

🍐 6

Fruits of Our Labour

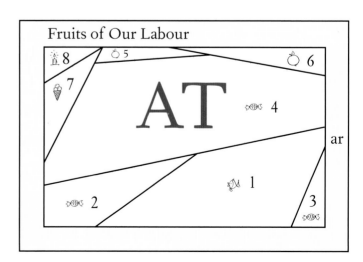

🕯 8

🍐 5

🍎 6

🍦 7

🍬 4

AT

ar

🐚 1

🍬 2

🍬 3

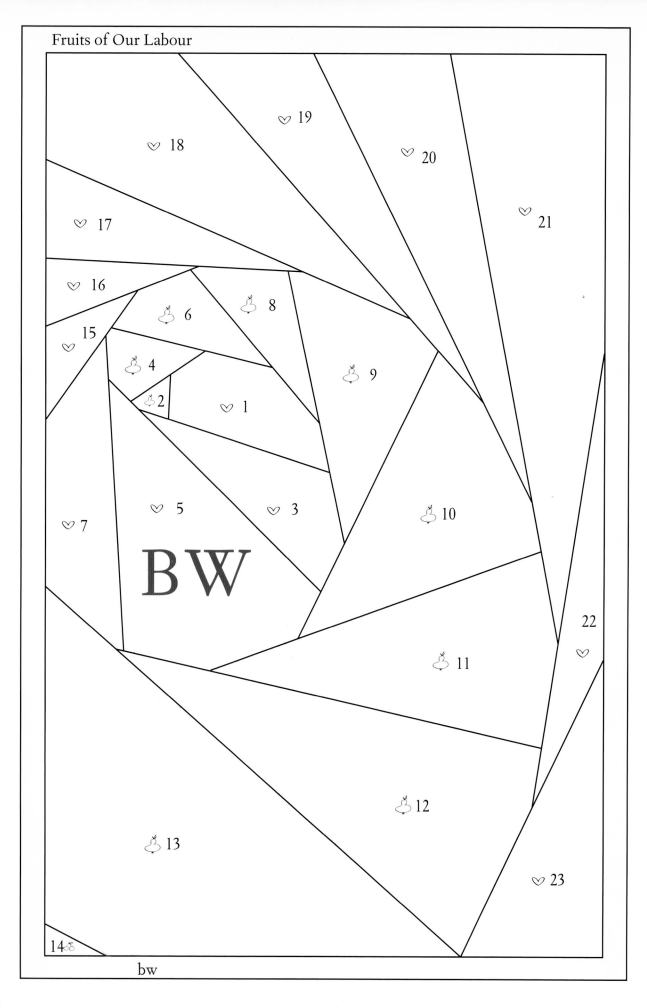

Fruits of our Labour

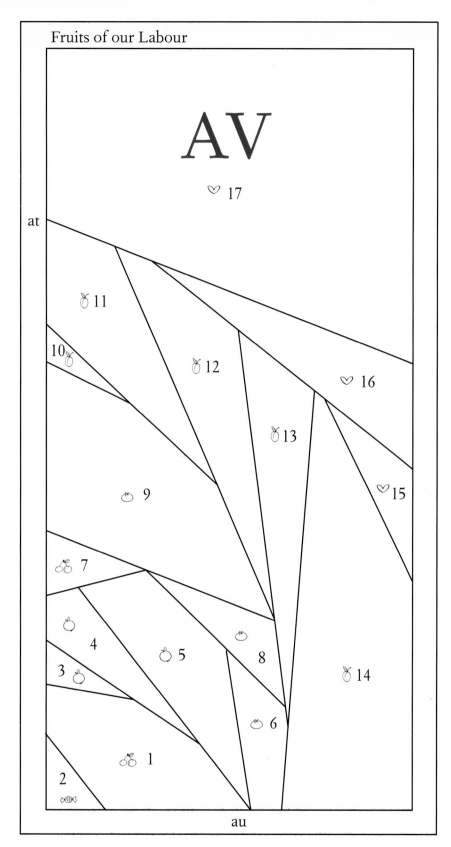

AV

♡ 17

at

🍐 11

10 🍊

🍐 12

♡ 16

🍐 13

🍅 9

♡ 15

🍒 7

🍎

4

🍎 5

🍅 8

🍐 14

3 🍎

🍅 6

🍒 1

2

🍬

au

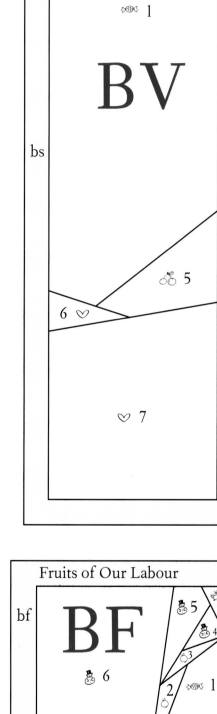

Fruits

bu

4 ☕

🍒 3

🍒 2

🍬 1

bs

BV

bx

🍒 5

6 ♡

♡ 7

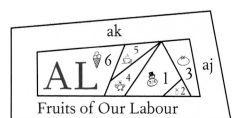

ak

AL 🍦 6

5

☕ 4

☕

🎩 1

🍅

3

🍬 2

aj

Fruits of Our Labour

Fruits

5 ♡

☕ 4

AH

🍅 2

🍅

3

af

🍦 1

ai

Fruits of Our Labour

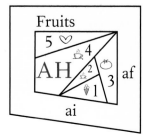

bf

BF

🎩 5

🍬 7

🎩 4

🍅 3

🎩 6

2

🍬 1

bd

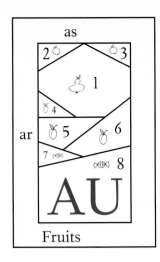

as
2 3
1
4
ar 5 6
7 8
AU
Fruits

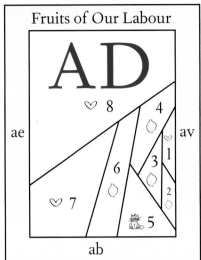

Fruits of Our Labour
AD
8
4
ae av
6 3 1
7 2
5
ab

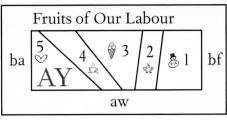

Fruits of Our Labour
ba 5 4 3 2 1 bf
AY
aw

1 4 6
aj 5 7
2 3 **AM**
Fruits of Our Labour

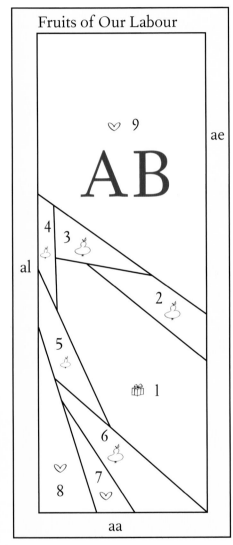

Fruits of Our Labour
9
AB
ae
4 3
2
al
5
1
6
8 7
aa

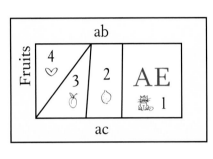

ab
4
3 2 **AE**
Fruits 1
ac

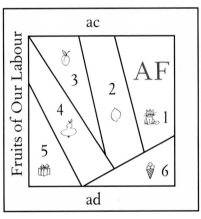

ac
3 2 **AF**
Fruits of Our Labour
4 1
5 6
ad

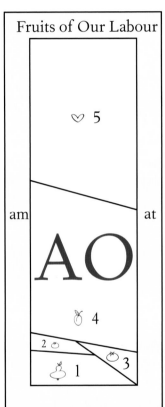

Fruits of Our Labour
5
AO
am at
4
2 1 3
aa

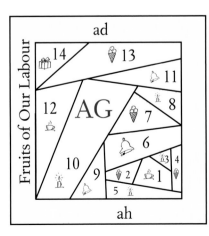

ad
14 13
11
12 **AG** 8
7
10 6
9 2 1 4 3
5
ah

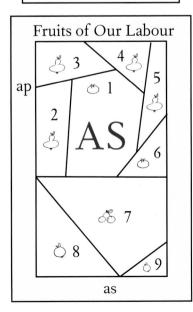

Fruits of Our Labour
3 4
1 5
ap 2 **AS**
6
7
8 9
as

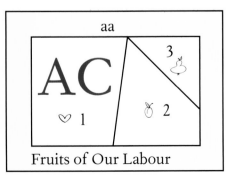

aa
AC 3
2
1
Fruits of Our Labour

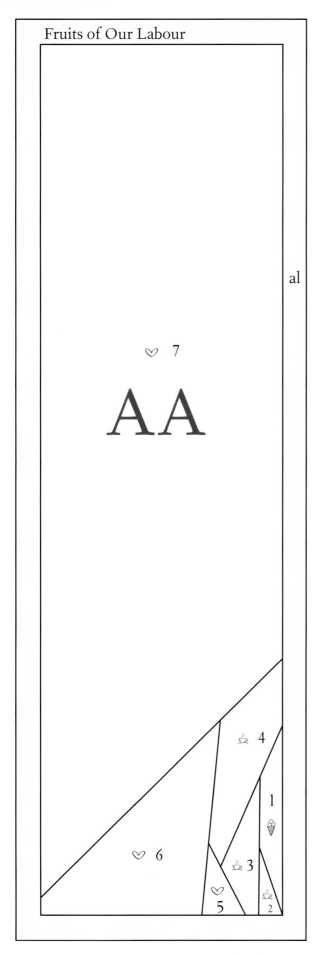

Fruits of Our Labour

AA

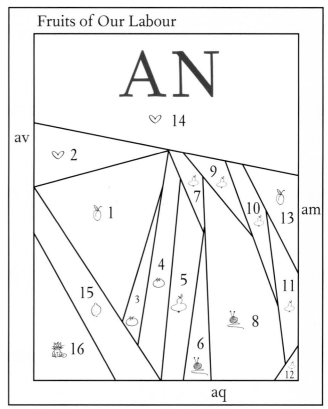

Fruits of Our Labour

AN

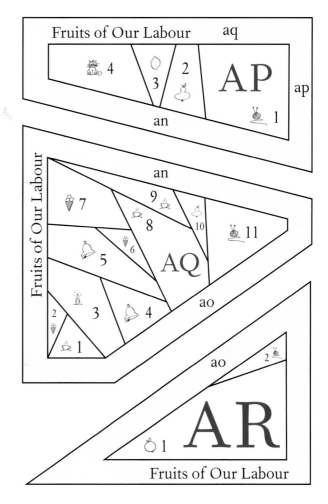

Fruits of Our Labour

AP

AQ

AR

Fruits of Our Labour

Holiday with Family

Finished Size: 42" x 36"
Rating: Challenging

A stately and elegant scene, *Holiday with Family* invokes warm memories of making snowmen, tossing snowballs, and sipping cocoa by the fire. This quilt is sure to be loved by your family and a welcome addition to your holiday decor.

Sewing this beautiful quilt is the culmination of your foundation piecing lessons. It may seem overwhelming at first, but just take it step-by-step.

Materials *(based on 40"-wide fabric)*
¼ yd. forest green
½ yd. sky blue
½ yd. white
½ yd. cream
⅛ yd. dark green
⅛ yd. medium green
⅛ yd. light green
¼ yd. yellow/gold
⅛ yd. dark slate blue
⅛ yd. medium slate blue
¼ yd. dark brown
¼ yd. medium brown
¼ yd. light brown
¼ yd. taupe
¼ yd. dark red
¼ yd. medium red
⅛ yd. light red
⅛ yd. flesh tone
⅛ yd. very dark gray
⅓ yd. dark gray
⅓ yd. medium gray
¼ yd. light gray
⅛ yd. magenta
⅛ yd. rose red
⅛ yd. pink
⅛ yd. black
1 yd. holiday print for crosswise cuts
    (or 1¼ yds. for lengthwise cuts)

Cutting *(for outside borders)*
From the holiday print, cut
    two 6½" x 30½" strips and
    two 6½" x 36½" strips.

Assembly
1. Sew units AA–DP using the Foundation Color Guide for color placement.

2. Baste around each unit within the ¼" seam allowance and trim.

3. Arrange all the units as shown in the Quilt Assembly Diagram. Flip the foundations over to the fabric side and check to see if you made any errors while sewing the units.

4. Turn the foundations back to the printed side. Matching the lowercase letters in the seam allowances, sew the units together in alphabetical order.

Borders
Sew the short border strips to the top and bottom of the quilt top. Add the remaining strips to the sides.

Finishing
1. Remove the paper from the back of the quilt top.

2. Layer the quilt top with batting and backing; baste.

3. Machine quilt the project, outlining the house, trees, sleigh, and horses.

4. Bind the quilt and add a hanging sleeve.

5. Sign and date your quilt.

Foundation Color Guide

 - forest green
 - sky blue
 - white
 - cream
 - dark green
 - medium green
 - light green
 - yellow/gold
 - dark slate blue
 - medium slate blue
 - dark brown
- medium brown
- light brown
- taupe
- dark red
- medium red
- light red
- flesh tone
 - very dark gray
 - dark gray
 - medium gray
 - light gray
 - magenta
- rose red
 - pink
 - black

Creative Options

Embellish the quilt and add fun details. Some
ideas inlude: adding jingle bells to the horse,
beaded ornaments on the tree inside the house,
and a wreath on the door.

Quilt Assembly Diagram

(view from printed side of foundation—border not shown)

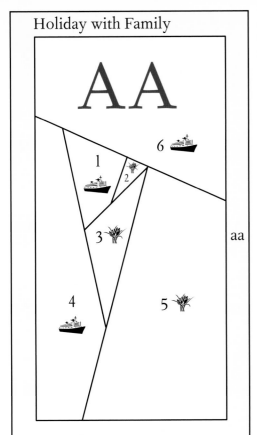

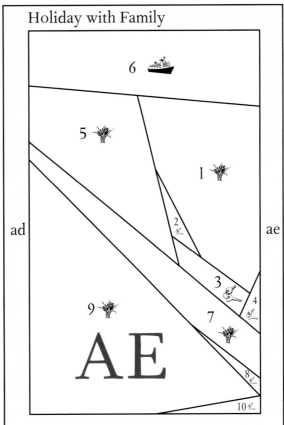

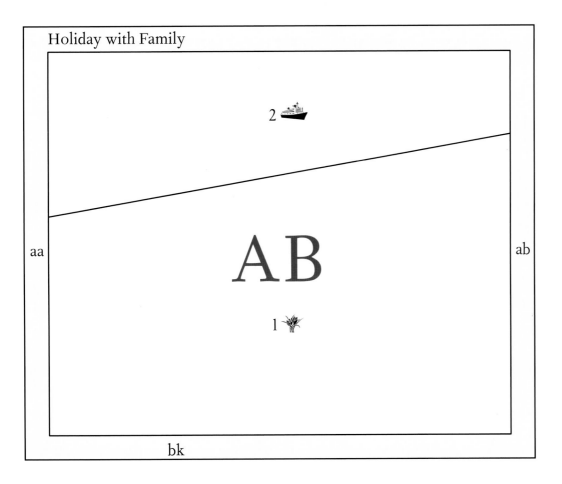

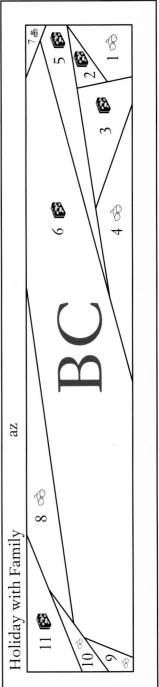

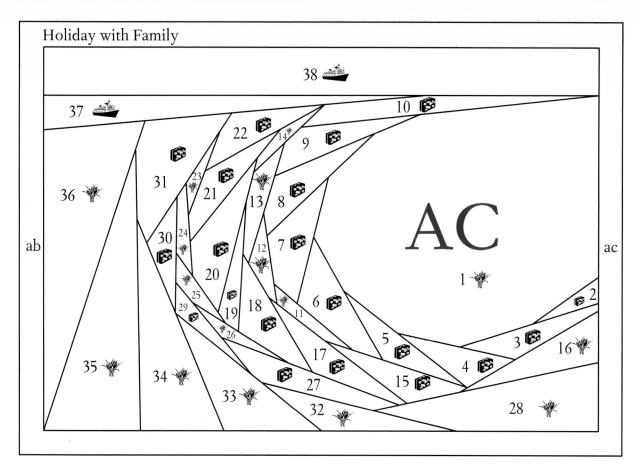

Holiday with Family

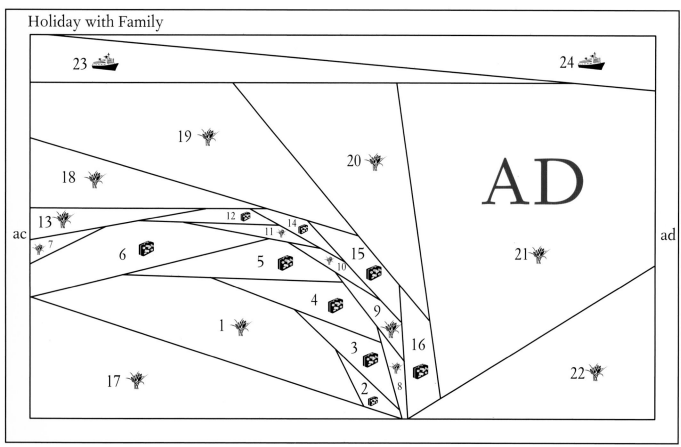

Holiday with Family

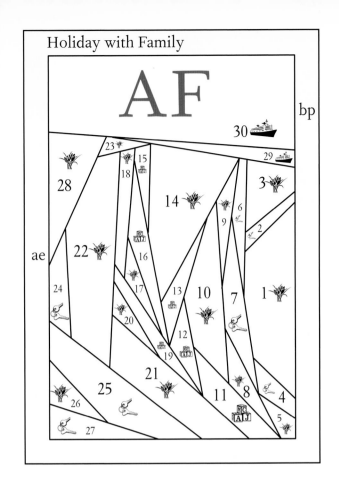

AF

bp

30

29

23
15
18
28
3
22
ae
14
6
9
2
16
24
17
13
10
7
1
20
12
19
11
25
21
8
26
4
27
5

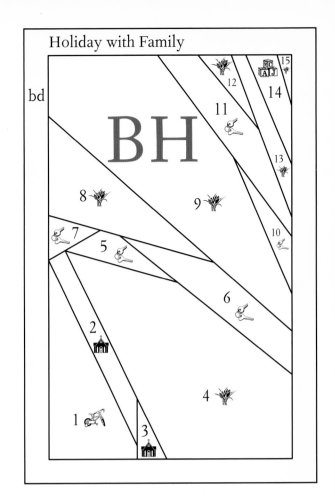

bd

BH

12
15
14
11
13
8
9
7
5
10
6
2
4
1
3

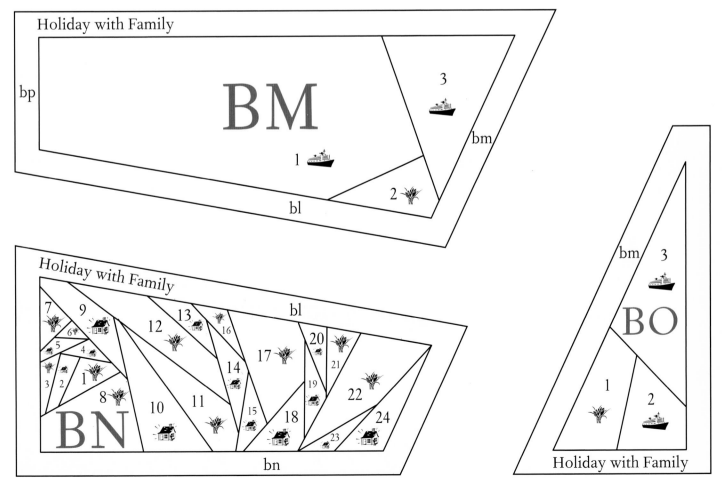

bp

BM

3

bm

1

2

bl

Holiday with Family

bl

7
9
13
12
16
5
6
17
20
4
14
21
3
2
1
19
22
8
10
11
15
18
24
23

BN

bn

bm
3

BO

1

2

Holiday with Family

97

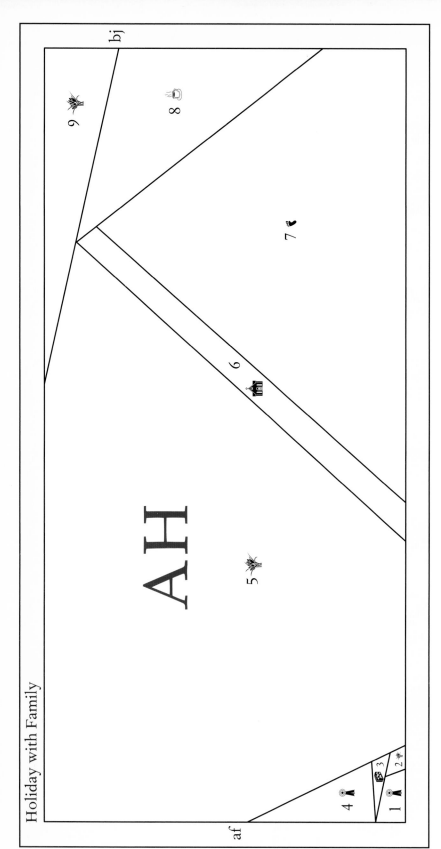

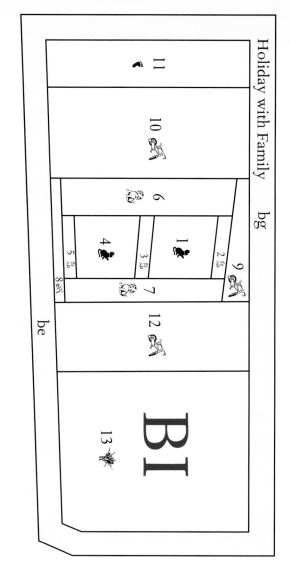

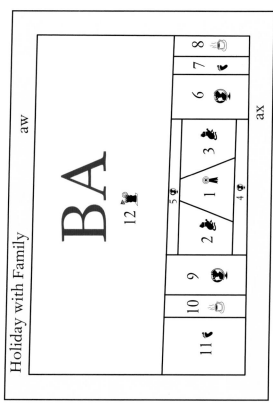

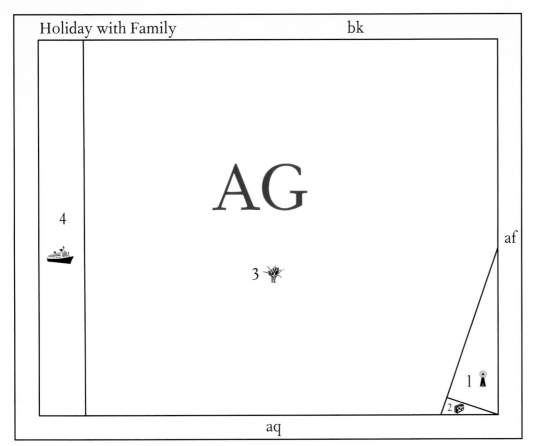
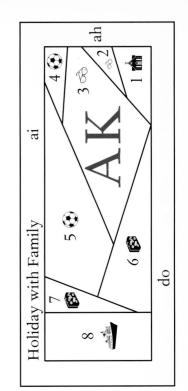
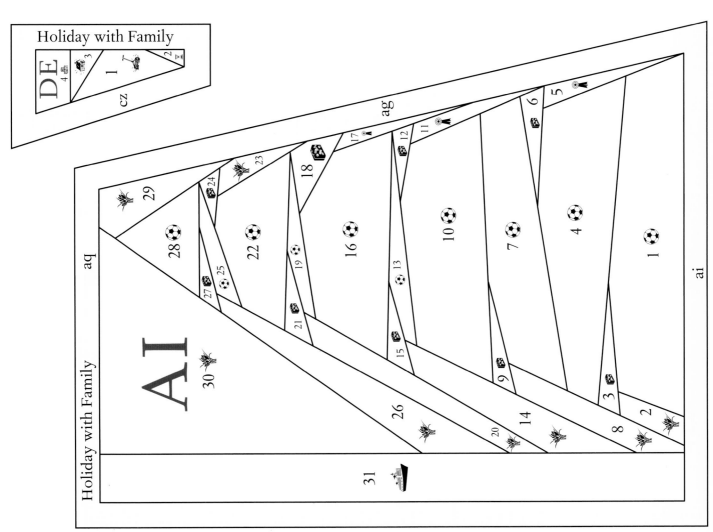

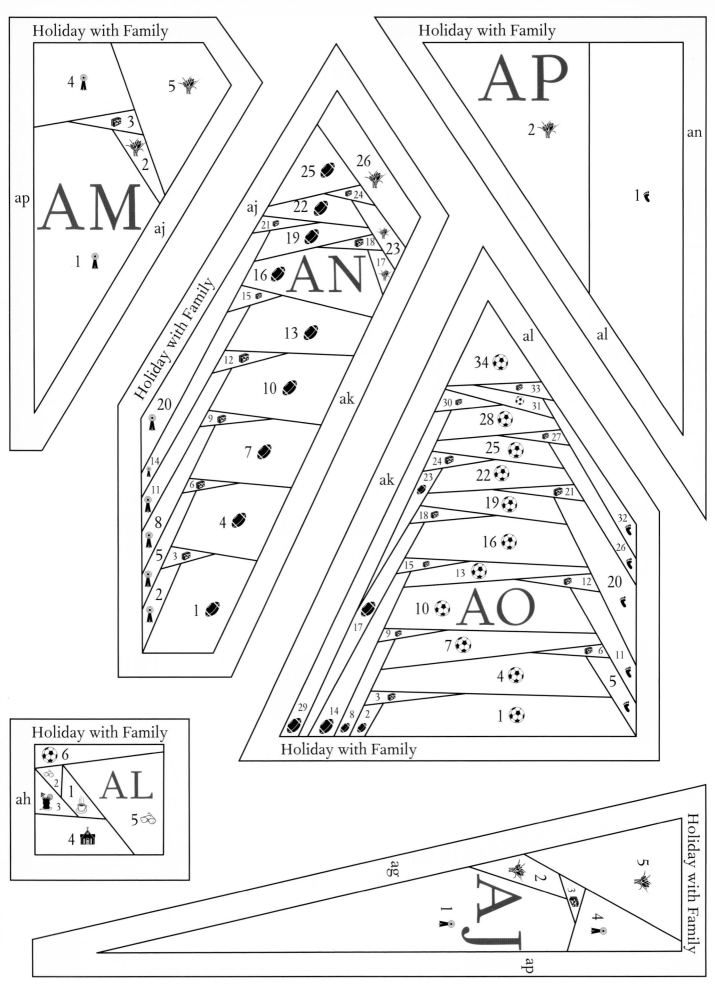

Holiday with Family

Holiday with Family

Holiday with Family

Holiday with Family

Holiday with Family

AM

AP

AN

AO

AL

AJ

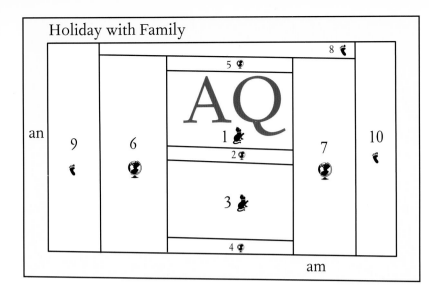

an

AQ

8

5

9 6 1 2 3 7 10

4

am

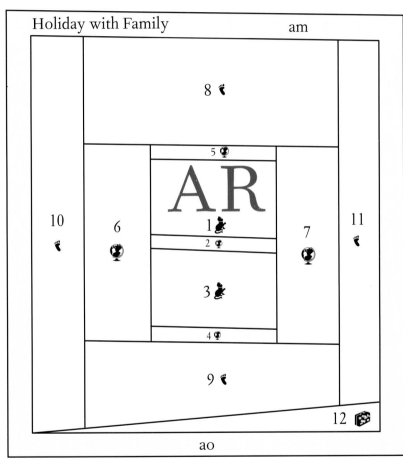

am

8

5

AR

10 6 1 2 3 7 11

4

9

12

ao

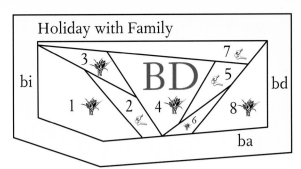

bi

3 BD 7 5 bd

1 2 4 6 8

ba

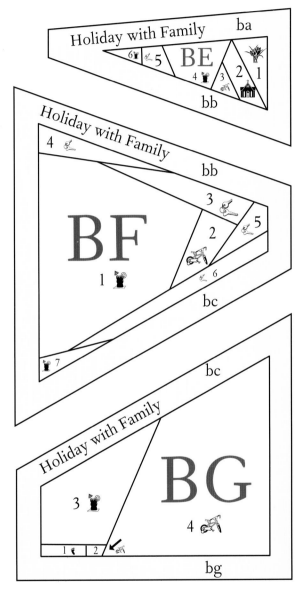

ba

6 5 BE 2 1

4 3

bb

4 bb

3

BF 2 5

1 6

7

bc

bc

BG

3

4

1 2

bg

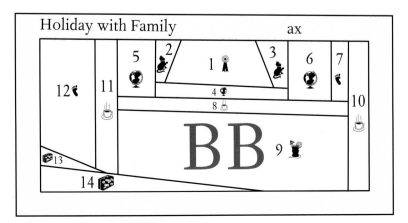

ax

2 3

5 1 6 7

12 11 4

8

10

BB

13 9

14

3

au 4 5 bi

1 AY

2 6

av

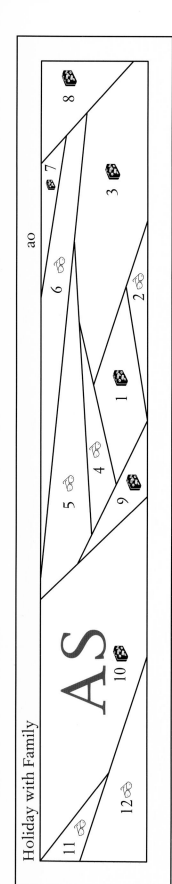

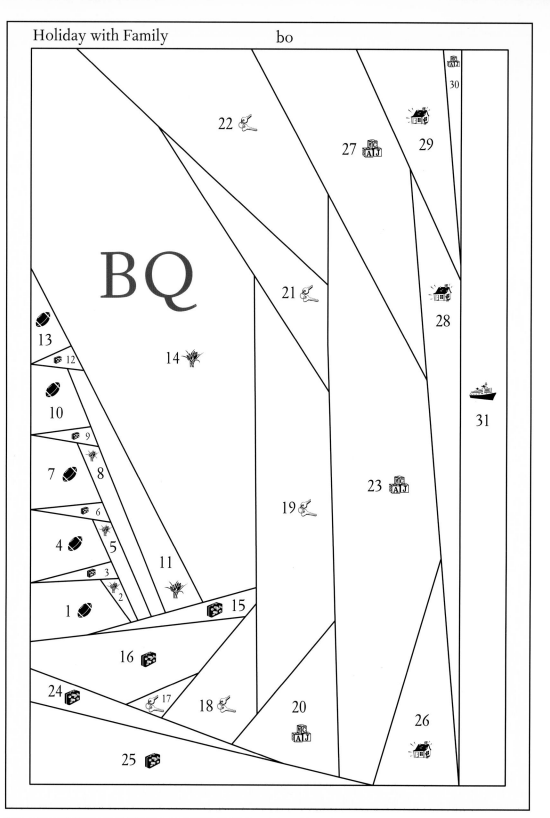

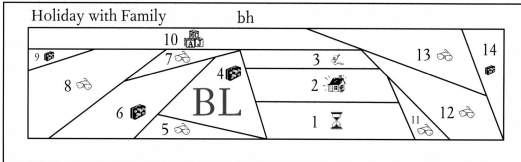

102

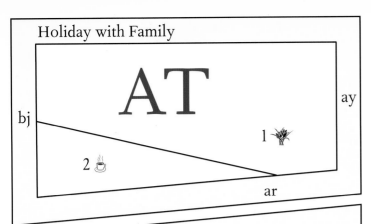

Holiday with Family

AT

bj

ay

1

2

ar

Holiday with Family

ar

AU

3

1

2

as

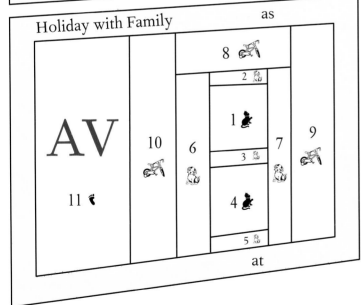

Holiday with Family

as

AV

10

6

7

9

8

2

1

3

4

5

11

at

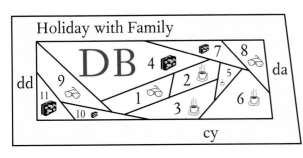

Holiday with Family

DB

dd

da

9

11

10

4

7

8

1

2

5

3

6

cy

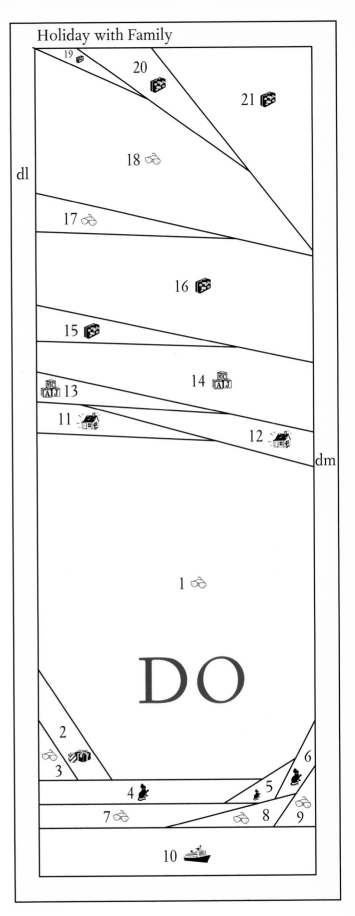

Holiday with Family

dl

19

20

21

18

17

16

15

14

13

11

12

dm

1

2

3

4

5

6

7

8

9

10

DO

103

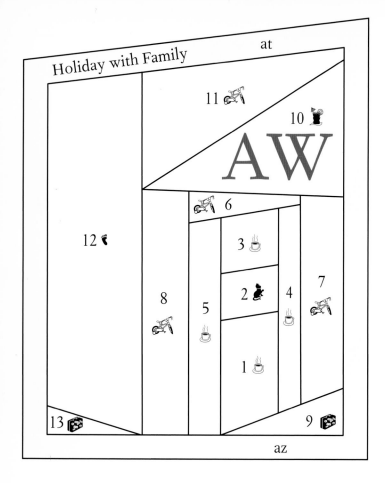

at

11

10

AW

6

3

12

2 4 7

8 5

1

13 9

az

4

3

ay AX au

2

1

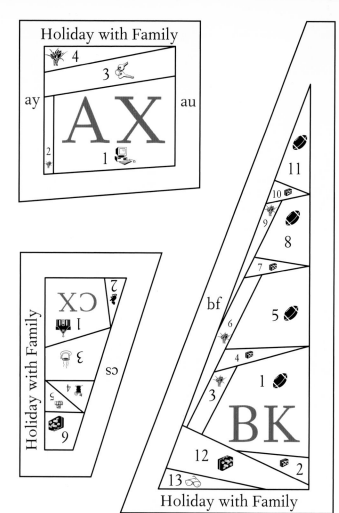

CX

1

3

4

5

6

Holiday with Family

bf

11

10

9

8

7

5

6

4

1

3

BK

12

13 2

Holiday with Family

av

AZ

12

9 2

1

7 11

3 8

4

5

6 10

aw

Holiday with Family

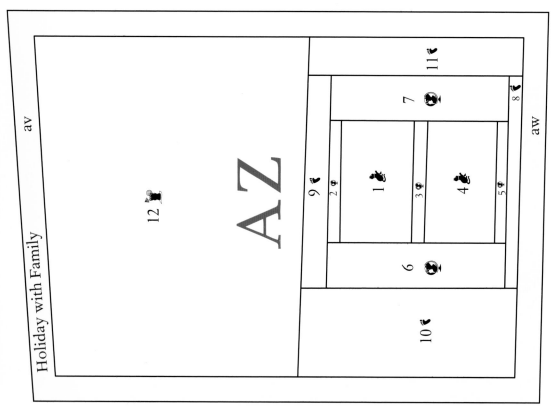

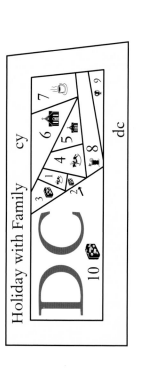

DC

cy

7

6

5 9

4

8

3

1

2

dc

10

Holiday with Family

104

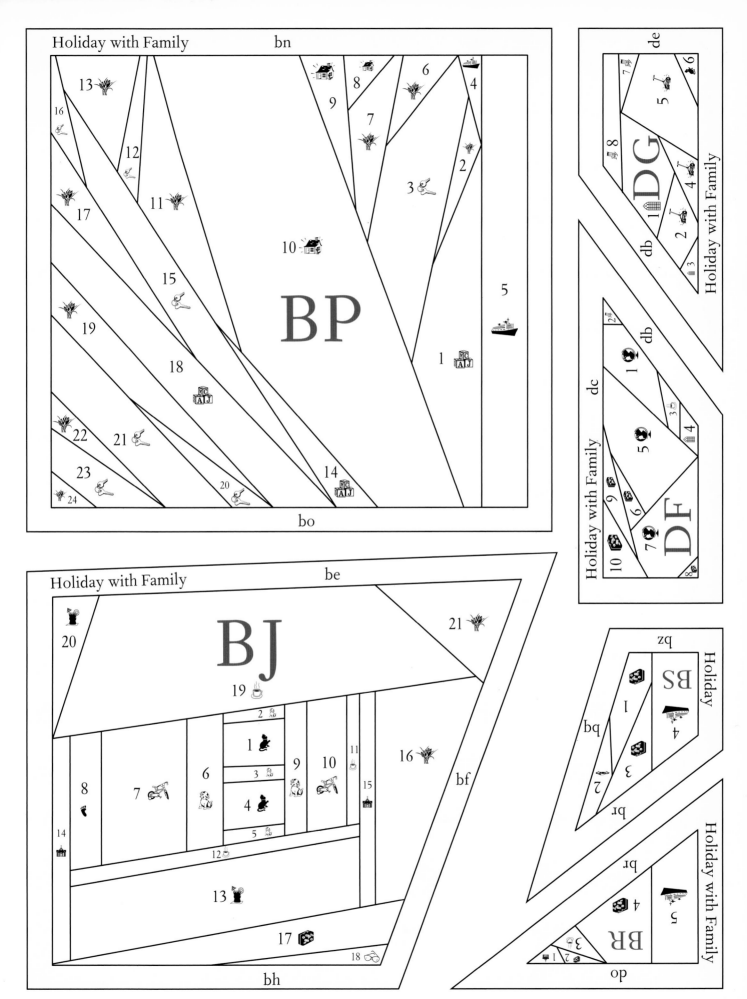

Holiday with Family

bn

13
16
12
17
11
10
BP
19
15
18
14
22
21
23
20
24
bo

Holiday with Family
be

20
BJ
21
19
16
8 7 6 1 9 10 11
2 3 4 5 12 15
14
13
17
18
bh
bf

Holiday with Family
de
DG
8
db
dc
Holiday with Family
DF
Holiday with Family

Holiday
bz
BS
bq
br
Holiday with Family
br
BR
bo

105

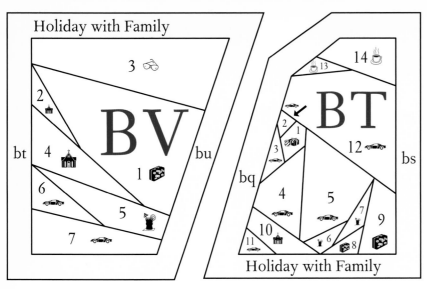
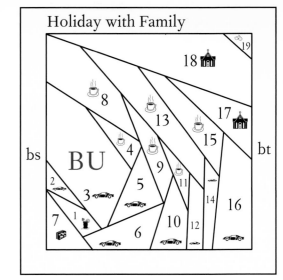
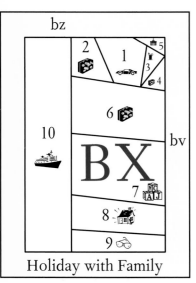
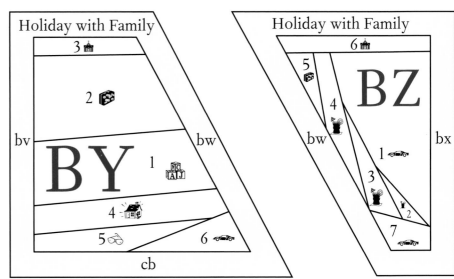
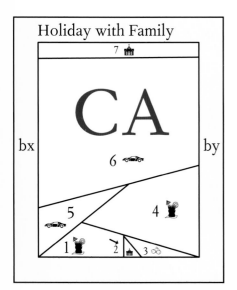
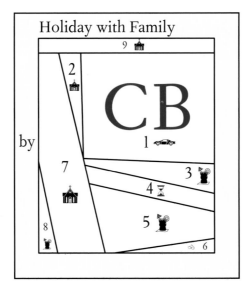
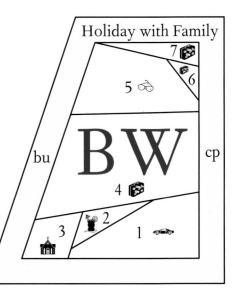

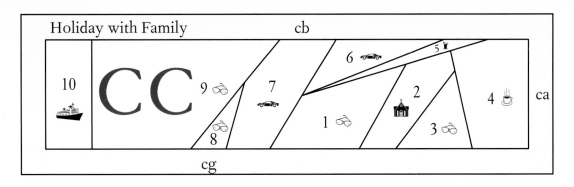

Holiday with Family

CC

cb

ca

cg

10 9 7 6 5 1 2 3 4 8

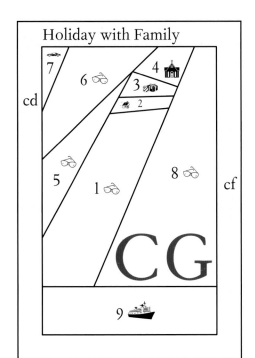

Holiday with Family

CG

cd

cf

7 6 4 3 2 5 1 8 9

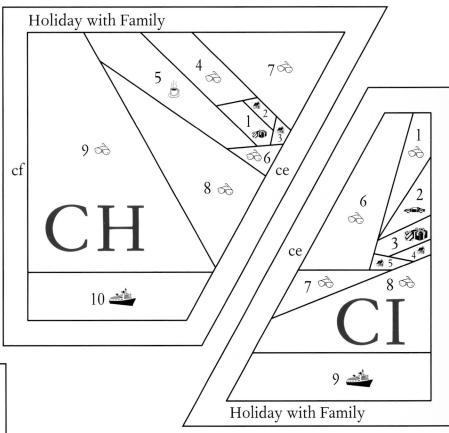

Holiday with Family

CH

cf

ce

ce

5 4 7 1 2 6 9 8 3 10

Holiday with Family

CI

1 2 6 3 4 5 7 8 9

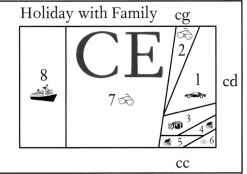

Holiday with Family

CE

cg

cd

cc

8 2 1 7 3 4 5 6

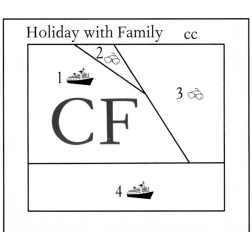

Holiday with Family

CF

cc

1 2 3 4

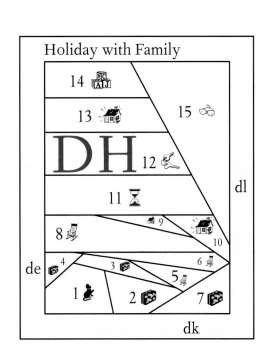

Holiday with Family

DH

dl

de

dk

14 13 15 12 11 9 8 10 4 3 6 1 2 5 7

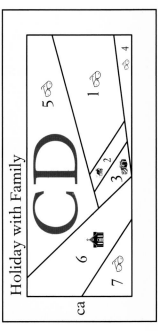

Holiday with Family

CD

ca

5 1 4 2 3 6 7

Holiday with Family

CJ
12, 9, 10, 11, cp, ch, 8, 3, 1, 2, 4, 6, 5, 7
cj

Holiday with Family

CW
9, 8, 12, 2, 11, cu, 10, 7, 1, cs, 6, 3, 4, 5
ct

Holiday with Family — cj

CL
9, 4, 5, 7, 3, 6, ci, 1, 2, 8

Holiday with Family

CM
9, 7, 8, ci, 5, 3, 6, 4, 2, 1
cm

Holiday with Family

CN
2, 7, 3, 1, 4, ck, 5, 6
co

Holiday with Family

CO
6, 4, ck, 1, 2, 5, cl, 3

Holiday with Family

CP
cm, 4, cl, 1, 3, 2

Holiday with Family — cn

CQ
co, 7, 2, 1, 3, 4, 5, 10, 11, 6, 8, 9

Holiday with Family — cw

CK
1, 2, 3
ch

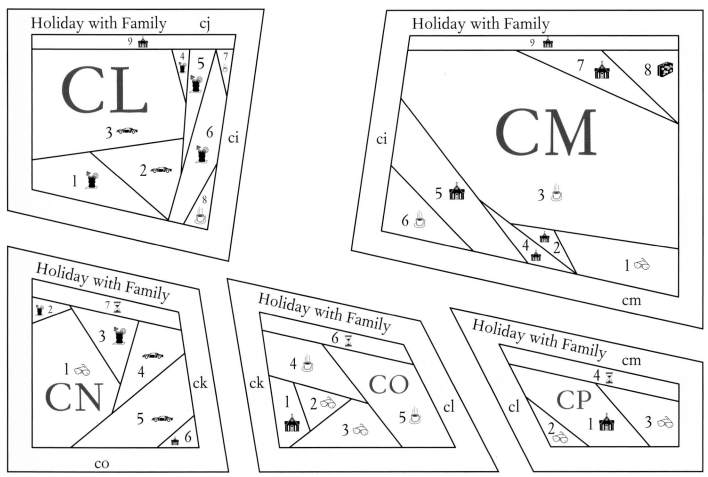
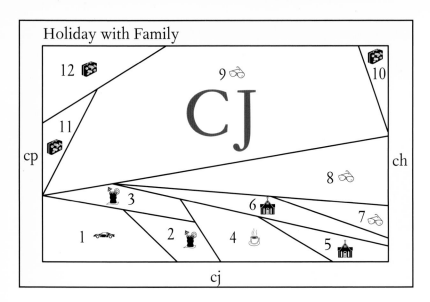
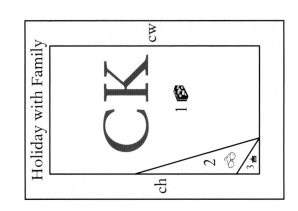
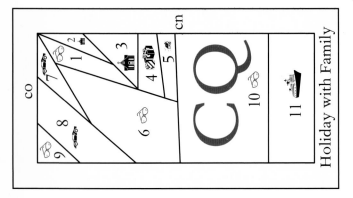
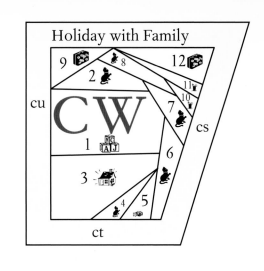

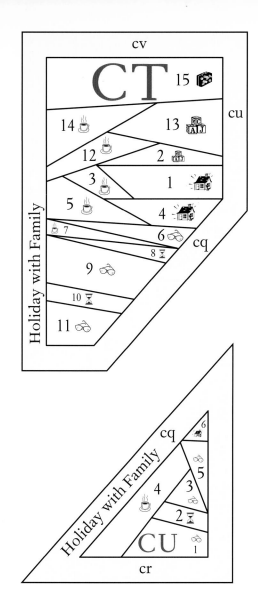

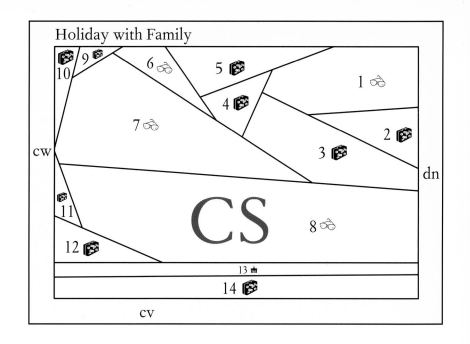

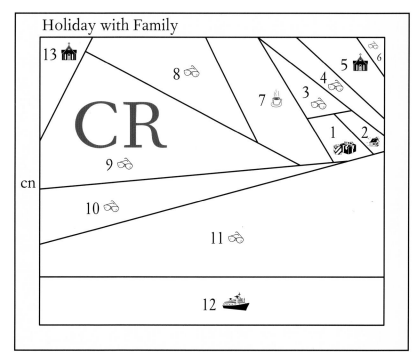

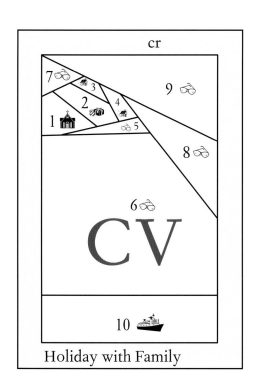

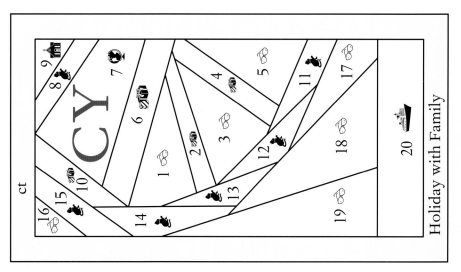

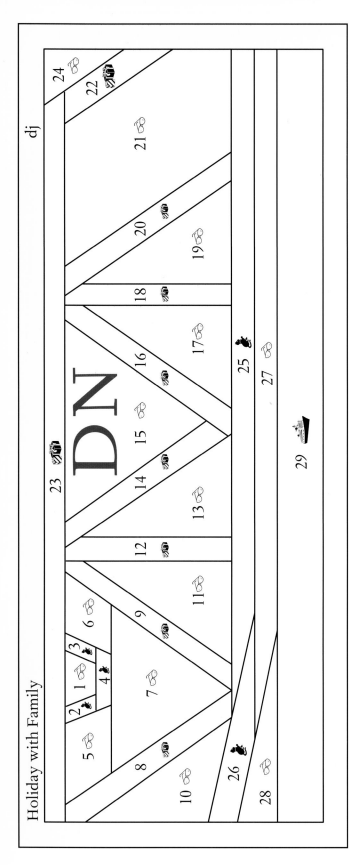

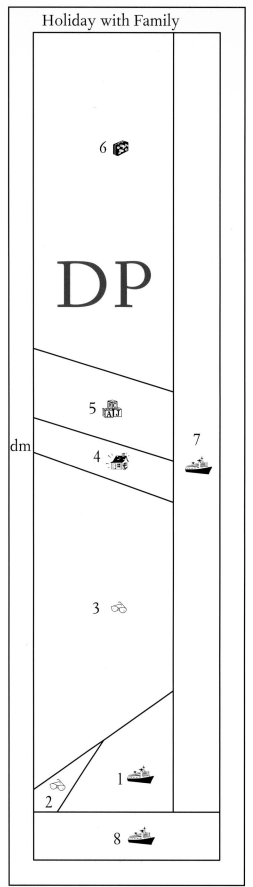

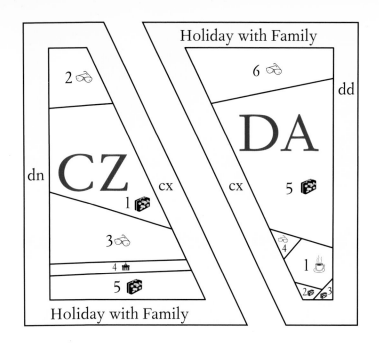
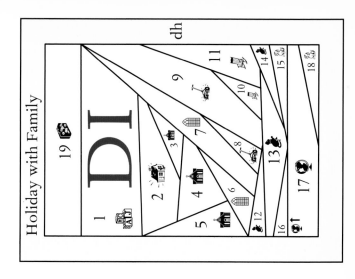
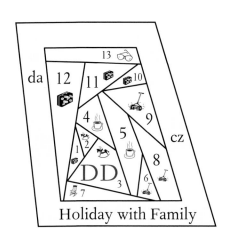
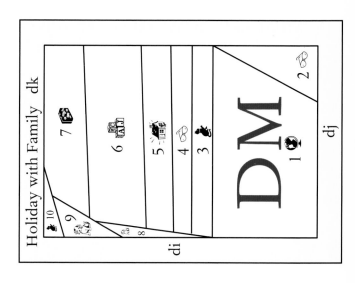
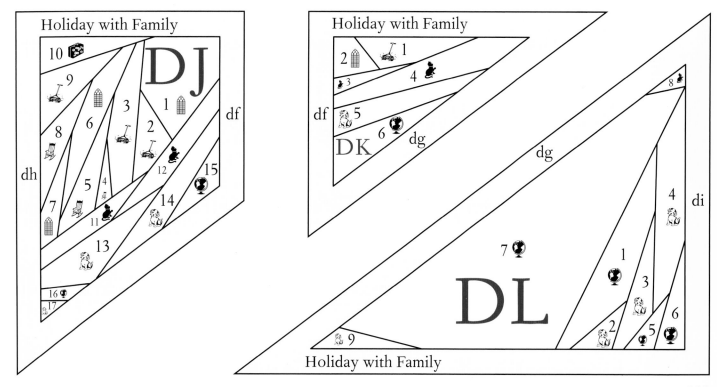

Martingale & Company
Toll-free: 1-800-426-3126

International: 1-425-483-3313
24-Hour Fax: 1-425-486-7596

PO Box 118, Bothell, WA 98041-0118 USA

Web site: www.patchwork.com
E-mail: info@martingale-pub.com

Books from

These books are available through your local quilt, fabric, craft-supply, or art-supply store. For more information, contact us for a free full-color catalog. You can also find our full catalog of books online at www.patchwork.com.

Appliqué
Appliqué for Baby
Appliqué in Bloom
Baltimore Bouquets
Basic Quiltmaking Techniques for Hand Appliqué
Basic Quiltmaking Techniques for Machine Appliqué
Coxcomb Quilt
The Easy Art of Appliqué
Folk Art Animals
Fun with Sunbonnet Sue
Garden Appliqué
The Nursery Rhyme Quilt
Red and Green: An Appliqué Tradition
Rose Sampler Supreme
Stars in the Garden
Sunbonnet Sue All Through the Year

Beginning Quiltmaking
Basic Quiltmaking Techniques for Borders & Bindings
Basic Quiltmaking Techniques for Curved Piecing
Basic Quiltmaking Techniques for Divided Circles
Basic Quiltmaking Techniques for Eight-Pointed Stars
Basic Quiltmaking Techniques for Hand Appliqué
Basic Quiltmaking Techniques for Machine Appliqué
Basic Quiltmaking Techniques for Strip Piecing
The Quilter's Handbook
Your First Quilt Book (or it should be!)

Crafts
15 Beads
Fabric Mosaics
Folded Fabric Fun
Making Memories

Cross-Stitch & Embroidery
Hand-Stitched Samplers from I Done My Best
Kitties to Stitch and Quilt: 15 Redwork Designs
Miniature Baltimore Album Quilts
A Silk-Ribbon Album

Designing Quilts
Color: The Quilter's Guide
Design Essentials: The Quilter's Guide
Design Your Own Quilts
Designing Quilts: The Value of Value
The Nature of Design
QuiltSkills
Sensational Settings
Surprising Designs from Traditional Quilt Blocks
Whimsies & Whynots

Holiday
Christmas Ribbonry
Easy Seasonal Wall Quilts
Favorite Christmas Quilts from That Patchwork Place
Holiday Happenings
Quilted for Christmas
Quilted for Christmas, Book IV
Special-Occasion Table Runners
Welcome to the North Pole

Home Decorating
The Home Decorator's Stamping Book
Make Room for Quilts
Special-Occasion Table Runners
Stitch & Stencil
Welcome Home: Debbie Mumm
Welcome Home: Kaffe Fassett

Knitting
Simply Beautiful Sweaters
Two Sticks and a String

Paper Arts
The Art of Handmade Paper and Collage
Grow Your Own Paper
Stamp with Style

Paper Piecing
Classic Quilts with Precise Foundation Piecing
Easy Machine Paper Piecing
Easy Mix & Match Machine Paper Piecing
Easy Paper-Pieced Keepsake Quilts
Easy Paper-Pieced Miniatures
Easy Reversible Vests
Go Wild with Quilts
Go Wild with Quilts—Again!
It's Raining Cats & Dogs
Mariner's Medallion
Needles and Notions
Paper-Pieced Curves
Paper Piecing the Seasons
A Quilter's Ark
Sewing on the Line
Show Me How to Paper Piece

Quilting & Finishing Techniques
The Border Workbook
Borders by Design
A Fine Finish
Happy Endings
Interlacing Borders
Lap Quilting Lives!
Loving Stitches
Machine Quilting Made Easy
Quilt It!
Quilting Design Sourcebook
Quilting Makes the Quilt
The Ultimate Book of Quilt Labels

Ribbonry
Christmas Ribbonry
A Passion for Ribbonry
Wedding Ribbonry

Rotary Cutting & Speed Piecing
101 Fabulous Rotary-Cut Quilts
365 Quilt Blocks a Year Perpetual Calendar
All-Star Sampler
Around the Block with Judy Hopkins
Basic Quiltmaking Techniques for Strip Piecing
Beyond Log Cabin
Block by Block
Easy Stash Quilts
Fat Quarter Quilts
The Joy of Quilting
A New Twist on Triangles
A Perfect Match
Quilters on the Go
ScrapMania
Shortcuts
Simply Scrappy Quilts
Spectacular Scraps
Square Dance
Stripples Strikes Again!
Strips That Sizzle
Surprising Designs from Traditional Quilt Blocks

Traditional Quilts with Painless Borders
Time-Crunch Quilts
Two-Color Quilts

Small & Miniature Quilts
Bunnies by the Bay Meets Little Quilts
Celebrate! With Little Quilts
Easy Paper-Pieced Miniatures
Fun with Miniature Log Cabin Blocks
Little Quilts all Through the House
Living with Little Quilts
Miniature Baltimore Album Quilts
A Silk-Ribbon Album
Small Quilts Made Easy
Small Wonders

Surface Design
Complex Cloth
Creative Marbling on Fabric
Dyes & Paints
Fantasy Fabrics
Hand-Dyed Fabric Made Easy
Jazz It Up
Machine Quilting with Decorative Threads
New Directions in Chenille
Thread Magic
Threadplay with Libby Lehman

Topics in Quiltmaking
Bargello Quilts
The Cat's Meow
Even More Quilts for Baby
Everyday Angels in Extraordinary Quilts
Fabric Collage Quilts
Fast-and-Fun Stenciled Quilts
Folk Art Quilts
It's Raining Cats & Dogs
Kitties to Stitch and Quilt: 15 Redwork Designs
Life in the Country with Country Threads
Machine-Stitched Cathedral Windows
More Quilts for Baby
A New Slant on Bargello Quilts
Patchwork Pantry
Pink Ribbon Quilts
Quilted Landscapes
The Quilted Nursery
Quilting Your Memories
Quilts for Baby
Quilts from Aunt Amy
Whimsies & Whynots

Watercolor Quilts
More Strip-Pieced Watercolor Magic
Quick Watercolor Quilts
Strip-Pieced Watercolor Magic
Watercolor Impressions
Watercolor Quilts

Wearables
Easy Reversible Vests
Just Like Mommy
New Directions in Chenille
Quick-Sew Fleece
Variations in Chenille